I WILL GO WITH THEE
AND BE THY GUIDE,
IN THY MOST NEED
TO GO BY THY SIDE

EVERYMAN'S LIBRARY
POCKET POETS

Shakespeare

Poems

EVERYMAN'S LIBRARY

POCKET POETS

Alfred A. Knopf · New York · Toronto

THIS IS A BORZOI BOOK

PUBLISHED BY ALFRED A. KNOPF, INC.

This selection by Graham Handley first published in Everyman's
Library, 1994
Copyright © 1994 by David Campbell Publishers Ltd.
Fifth printing

ISBN 0-679-43320-1
LC 94-2494

Library of Congress Cataloging-in-Publication Data
Shakespeare, William, 1564–1616.
[Poems]
Poems / William Shakespeare.
p.   cm.—(Everyman's library pocket poets)
Includes bibliographical references.
ISBN 0-679-43320-1
I. Title. II. Series.

PR2841   1994   94-2494
821'.3—dc20   CIP

Typography by Peter B. Willberg

Typeset in the UK by MS Filmsetting Ltd., Frome, Somerset

Printed and bound in Germany
by Graphischer Grossbetrieb Pössneck GmbH

WILLIAM SHAKESPEARE

CONTENTS

SONNETS

From fairest creatures we desire increase,
That thereby beauty's rose might never die,
But as the riper should by time decease,
His tender heir might bear his memory;
But thou contracted to thine own bright eyes,
Feed'st thy light's flame with self-substantial fuel,
Making a famine where abundance lies,
Thyself thy foe, to thy sweet self too cruel.
Thou that art now the world's fresh ornament,
And only herald to the gaudy spring,
Within thine own bud buriest thy content,
And, tender churl, mak'st waste in niggarding.
    Pity the world, or else this glutton be,
    To eat the world's due, by the grave and thee.

When forty winters shall besiege thy brow,
And dig deep trenches in thy beauty's field,
Thy youth's proud livery, so gazed on now,
Will be a tottered weed of small worth held:
Then being asked where all thy beauty lies,
Where all the treasure of thy lusty days,
To say within thine own deep-sunken eyes,
Were an all-eating shame and thriftless praise.
How much more praise deserved thy beauty's use,
If thou couldst answer, "This fair child of mine
Shall sum my count, and make my old excuse,"
Proving his beauty by succession thine.
    This were to be new made when thou art old,
    And see thy blood warm when thou feel'st it cold.

Look in thy glass and tell the face thou viewest
Now is the time that face should form another,
Whose fresh repair if now thou not renewest,
Thou dost beguile the world, unbless some mother.
For where is she so fair whose uneared womb
Disdains the tillage of thy husbandry?
Or who is he so fond will be the tomb
Of his self-love to stop posterity?
Thou art thy mother's glass, and she in thee
Calls back the lovely April of her prime;
So thou through windows of thine age shalt see,
Despite of wrinkles, this thy golden time.
　　But if thou live rememb'red not to be,
　　Die single and thine image dies with thee.

Unthrifty loveliness, why dost thou spend
Upon thyself thy beauty's legacy?
Nature's bequest gives nothing but doth lend,
And being frank she lends to those are free.
Then, beauteous niggard, why dost thou abuse
The bounteous largess given thee to give?
Profitless usurer, why dost thou use
So great a sum of sums yet canst not live?
For having traffic with thyself alone,
Thou of thyself thy sweet self dost deceive.
Then how when Nature calls thee to be gone,
What acceptable audit canst thou leave?
   Thy unused beauty must be tombed with thee,
   Which, usèd, lives th' executor to be.

Those hours that with gentle work did frame
The lovely gaze where every eye doth dwell
Will play the tyrants to the very same
And that unfair which fairly doth excel;
For never-resting Time leads summer on
To hideous winter and confounds him there,
Sap checked with frost and lusty leaves quite gone,
Beauty o'ersnowed and bareness everywhere.
Then, were not summer's distillation left
A liquid prisoner pent in walls of glass,
Beauty's effect with beauty were bereft,
Nor it nor no remembrance what it was.
  But flowers distilled though they with winter meet,
  Leese but their show, their substance still lives sweet.

Then let not winter's ragged hand deface
In thee thy summer ere thou be distilled.
Make sweet some vial; treasure thou some place
With beauty's treasure ere it be self-killed.
That use is not forbidden usury
Which happies those that pay the willing loan;
That's for thyself to breed another thee,
Or ten times happier be it ten for one.
Ten times thyself were happier than thou art,
If ten of thine ten times refigured thee:
Then what could death do if thou shouldst depart,
Leaving thee living in posterity?
   Be not self-willed, for thou art much too fair,
    To be death's conquest and make worms thine heir.

Lo, in the orient when the gracious light
Lifts up his burning head, each under eye
Doth homage to his new-appearing sight,
Serving with looks his sacred majesty;
And having climbed the steep-up heavenly hill,
Resembling strong youth in his middle age,
Yet mortal looks adore his beauty still,
Attending on his golden pilgrimage;
But when from highmost pitch, with weary car,
Like feeble age he reeleth from the day,
The eyes, 'fore duteous, now converted are
From his low tract and look another way:
   So thou, thyself outgoing in thy noon,
   Unlooked on diest unless thou get a son.

Music to hear, why hear'st thou music sadly?
Sweets with sweets war not, joy delights in joy.
Why lov'st thou that which thou receiv'st not gladly,
Or else receiv'st with pleasure thine annoy?
If the true concord of well tunèd sounds,
By unions married, do offend thine ear,
They do but sweetly chide thee, who confounds
In singleness the parts that thou shouldst bear.
Mark how one string, sweet husband to another,
Strikes each in each by mutual ordering;
Resembling sire, and child, and happy mother,
Who all in one, one pleasing note do sing;
　　Whose speechless song, being many, seeming one,
　　Sings this to thee, "Thou single wilt prove none."

Is it for fear to wet a widow's eye
That thou consum'st thyself in single life?
Ah, if thou issueless shalt hap to die,
The world will wail thee like a makeless wife;
The world will be thy widow and still weep,
That thou no form of thee hast left behind,
When every private widow well may keep,
By children's eyes, her husband's shape in mind.
Look what an unthrift in the world doth spend,
Shifts but his place, for still the world enjoys it;
But beauty's waste hath in the world an end,
And kept unused, the user so destroys it:
   No love toward others in that bosom sits
   That on himself such murd'rous shame commits.

For shame, deny that thou bear'st love to any
Who for thyself art so unprovident.
Grant if thou wilt, thou art beloved of many,
But that thou none lov'st is most evident;
For thou art so possessed with murd'rous hate,
That 'gainst thyself thou stick'st not to conspire,
Seeking that beauteous roof to ruinate,
Which to repair should be thy chief desire.
O, change thy thought, that I may change my mind.
Shall hate be fairer lodged than gentle love?
Be as thy presence is, gracious and kind,
Or to thyself at least kind-hearted prove.
    Make thee another self for love of me,
      That beauty still may live in thine or thee.

As fast as thou shalt wane, so fast thou grow'st
In one of thine, from that which thou departest;
And that fresh blood which youngly thou bestow'st
Thou mayst call thine, when thou from youth convertest.
Herein lives wisdom, beauty, and increase;
Without this, folly, age, and cold decay.
If all were minded so, the times should cease,
And threescore year would make the world away.
Let those whom Nature hath not made for store,
Harsh, featureless, and rude, barrenly perish.
Look whom she best endowed, she gave the more;
Which bounteous gift thou shouldst in bounty cherish.
   She carved thee for her seal, and meant thereby
   Thou shouldst print more, not let that copy die.

When I do count the clock that tells the time,
And see the brave day sunk in hideous night;
When I behold the violet past prime,
And sable curls are silvered o'er with white;
When lofty trees I see barren of leaves,
Which erst from heat did canopy the herd,
And summer's green, all girded up in sheaves,
Borne on the bier with white and bristly beard;
Then of thy beauty do I question make,
That thou among the wastes of time must go,
Since sweets and beauties do themselves forsake,
And die as fast as they see others grow,
    And nothing 'gainst Time's scythe can make defense,
    Save breed, to brave him when he takes thee hence.

O, that you were yourself, but, love, you are
No longer yours than you yourself here live;
Against this coming end you should prepare,
And your sweet semblance to some other give.
So should that beauty which you hold in lease
Find no determination, then you were
Yourself again after your self's decease,
When your sweet issue your sweet form should bear.
Who lets so fair a house fall to decay,
Which husbandry in honor might uphold
Against the stormy gusts of winter's day
And barren rage of death's eternal cold?
    O, none but unthrifts! Dear my love, you know,
    You had a father; let your son say so.

Not from the stars do I my judgment pluck,
And yet methinks I have astronomy;
But not to tell of good or evil luck,
Of plagues, of dearths, or seasons' quality;
Nor can I fortune to brief minutes tell,
Pointing to each his thunder, rain, and wind,
Or say with princes if it shall go well
By oft predict that I in heaven find.
But from thine eyes my knowledge I derive,
And, constant stars, in them I read such art
As truth and beauty shall together thrive
If from thyself to store thou wouldst convert:
    Or else of thee this I prognosticate,
    Thy end is truth's and beauty's doom and date.

When I consider everything that grows
Holds in perfection but a little moment,
That this huge stage presenteth naught but shows
Whereon the stars in secret influence comment;
When I perceive that men as plants increase,
Cheerèd and checked even by the selfsame sky,
Vaunt in their youthful sap, at height decrease,
And wear their brave state out of memory;
Then the conceit of this inconstant stay
Sets you most rich in youth before my sight,
Where wasteful Time debateth with Decay,
To change your day of youth to sullied night;
    And, all in war with Time for love of you,
    As he takes from you, I engraft you new.

Who will believe my verse in time to come
If it were filled with your most high deserts?
Though yet heaven knows it is but as a tomb
Which hides your life and shows not half your parts.
If I could write the beauty of your eyes,
And in fresh numbers number all your graces,
The age to come would say "This poet lies,
Such heavenly touches ne'er touched earthly faces."
So should my papers, yellowed with their age,
Be scorned, like old men of less truth than tongue,
And your true rights be termed a poet's rage
And stretchèd meter of an antique song:
    But were some child of yours alive that time,
    You should live twice, in it and in my rhyme.

Shall I compare thee to a summer's day?
Thou art more lovely and more temperate.
Rough winds do shake the darling buds of May,
And summer's lease hath all too short a date.
Sometime too hot the eye of heaven shines,
And often is his gold complexion dimmed;
And every fair from fair sometime declines,
By chance, or nature's changing course, untrimmed;
But thy eternal summer shall not fade,
Nor lose possession of that fair thou ow'st,
Nor shall Death brag thou wand'rest in his shade,
When in eternal lines to time thou grow'st.
   So long as men can breathe or eyes can see,
   So long lives this, and this gives life to thee.

Devouring Time, blunt thou the lion's paws,
And make the earth devour her own sweet brood;
Pluck the keen teeth from the fierce tiger's jaws,
And burn the long-lived phœnix in her blood;
Make glad and sorry seasons as thou fleets,
And do whate'er thou wilt, swift-footed Time,
To the wide world and all her fading sweets;
But I forbid thee one most heinous crime,
O, carve not with thy hours my love's fair brow,
Nor draw no lines there with thine antique pen.
Him in thy course untainted do allow,
For beauty's pattern to succeeding men.
 Yet do thy worst, old Time; despite thy wrong,
 My love shall in my verse ever live young.

A woman's face, with Nature's own hand painted,
Hast thou, the master mistress of my passion;
A woman's gentle heart, but not acquainted
With shifting change, as is false women's fashion;
An eye more bright than theirs, less false in rolling,
Gilding the object whereupon it gazeth;
A man in hue all hues in his controlling,
Which steals men's eyes and women's souls amazeth.
And for a woman wert thou first created,
Till Nature as she wrought thee fell a-doting,
And by addition me of thee defeated,
By adding one thing to my purpose nothing.
  But since she pricked thee out for women's pleasure,
  Mine be thy love, and thy love's use their treasure.

So is it not with me as with that Muse,
Stirred by a painted beauty to his verse,
Who heaven itself for ornament doth use,
And every fair with his fair doth rehearse;
Making a couplement of proud compare
With sun and moon, with earth and sea's rich gems,
With April's first-born flowers, and all things rare
That heaven's air in this huge rondure hems.
O, let me true in love but truly write,
And then believe me, my love is as fair
As any mother's child, though not so bright
As those gold candles fixed in heaven's air:
    Let them say more that like of hearsay well;
    I will not praise that purpose not to sell.

My glass shall not persuade me I am old,
So long as youth and thou are of one date,
But when in thee Time's furrows I behold,
Then look I death my days should expiate.
For all that beauty that doth cover thee
Is but the seemly raiment of my heart,
Which in thy breast doth live, as thine in me.
How can I then be elder than thou art?
O, therefore, love, be of thyself so wary
As I, not for myself, but for thee will,
Bearing thy heart, which I will keep so chary
As tender nurse her babe from faring ill.
    Presume not on thy heart when mine is slain;
    Thou gav'st me thine, not to give back again.

As an unperfect actor on the stage,
Who with his fear is put besides his part,
Or some fierce thing replete with too much rage,
Whose strength's abundance weakens his own heart;
So I, for fear of trust, forget to say
The perfect ceremony of love's right,
And in mine own love's strength seem to decay,
O'ercharged with burden of mine own love's might.
O, let my books be then the eloquence
And dumb presagers of my speaking breast,
Who plead for love, and look for recompense,
More than that tongue that more hath more expressed.
　　O, learn to read what silent love hath writ.
　　To hear with eyes belongs to love's fine wit.

Mine eye hath played the painter and hath steeled
Thy beauty's form in table of my heart;
My body is the frame wherein 'tis held,
And perspective it is best painter's art,
For through the painter must you see his skill,
To find where your true image pictured lies,
Which in my bosom's shop is hanging still,
That hath his windows glazèd with thine eyes.
Now see what good turns eyes for eyes have done:
Mine eyes have drawn thy shape, and thine for me
Are windows to my breast, wherethrough the sun
Delights to peep, to gaze therein on thee.
    Yet eyes this cunning want to grace their art,
    They draw but what they see, know not the heart.

Weary with toil, I haste me to my bed,
The dear repose for limbs with travel tired,
But then begins a journey in my head
To work my mind when body's work's expired;
For then my thoughts, from far where I abide,
Intend a zealous pilgrimage to thee,
And keep my drooping eyelids open wide,
Looking on darkness which the blind do see;
Save that my soul's imaginary sight
Presents thy shadow to my sightless view,
Which like a jewel hung in ghastly night,
Makes black night beauteous and her old face new.
  Lo, thus, by day my limbs, by night my mind,
    For thee, and for myself, no quiet find.

How can I then return in happy plight
That am debarred the benefit of rest,
When day's oppression is not eased by night,
But day by night and night by day oppressed,
And each, though enemies to either's reign,
Do in consent shake hands to torture me,
The one by toil, the other to complain
How far I toil, still farther off from thee?
I tell the day, to please him, thou art bright
And dost him grace when clouds do blot the heaven;
So flatter I the swart-complexioned night,
When sparkling stars twire not, thou gild'st the even.
  But day doth daily draw my sorrows longer,
    And night doth nightly make grief's length seem
      stronger.

When, in disgrace with Fortune and men's eyes,
I all alone beweep my outcast state,
And trouble deaf heaven with my bootless cries,
And look upon myself and curse my fate,
Wishing me like to one more rich in hope,
Featured like him, like him with friends possessed,
Desiring this man's art, and that man's scope,
With what I most enjoy contented least;
Yet in these thoughts myself almost despising,
Haply I think on thee, and then my state,
Like to the lark at break of day arising
From sullen earth, sings hymns at heaven's gate;
    For thy sweet love rememb'red such wealth brings,
    That then I scorn to change my state with kings.

When to the sessions of sweet silent thought
I summon up remembrance of things past,
I sigh the lack of many a thing I sought,
And with old woes new wail my dear Time's waste.
Then can I drown an eye, unused to flow,
For precious friends hid in death's dateless night,
And weep afresh love's long since canceled woe,
And moan th' expense of many a vanished sight;
Then can I grieve at grievances foregone,
And heavily from woe to woe tell o'er
The sad account of fore-bemoanèd moan,
Which I new pay as if not paid before.
    But if the while I think on thee, dear friend,
     All losses are restored and sorrows end.

If thou survive my well-contented day,
When that churl Death my bones with dust shall cover,
And shalt by fortune once more resurvey
These poor rude lines of thy deceasèd lover,
Compare them with the bett'ring of the time,
And though they be outstripped by every pen,
Reserve them for my love, not for their rhyme,
Exceeded by the height of happier men.
O, then vouchsafe me but this loving thought:
"Had my friend's Muse grown with this growing age,
A dearer birth than this his love had brought,
To march in ranks of better equipage;
      But since he died, and poets better prove,
      Theirs for their style I'll read, his for his love."

Full many a glorious morning have I seen
Flatter the mountain tops with sovereign eye,
Kissing with golden face the meadows green,
Gilding pale streams with heavenly alchemy;
Anon permit the basest clouds to ride
With ugly rack on his celestial face,
And from the forlorn world his visage hide,
Stealing unseen to west with this disgrace.
Even so my sun one early morn did shine,
With all triumphant splendor on my brow;
But out alack, he was but one hour mine,
The region cloud hath masked him from me now.
    Yet him for this my love no whit disdaineth;
    Suns of the world may stain when heaven's
        sun staineth.

Why didst thou promise such a beauteous day,
And make me travel forth without my cloak,
To let base clouds o'ertake me in my way,
Hiding thy brav'ry in their rotten smoke?
'Tis not enough that through the cloud thou break,
To dry the rain on my storm-beaten face,
For no man well of such a salve can speak,
That heals the wound, and cures not the disgrace.
Nor can thy shame give physic to my grief;
Though thou repent, yet I have still the loss.
Th' offender's sorrow lends but weak relief
To him that bears the strong offense's cross.
    Ah, but those tears are pearl which thy love sheeds,
    And they are rich and ransom all ill deeds.

No more be grieved at that which thou hast done:
Roses have thorns, and silver fountains mud,
Clouds and eclipses stain both moon and sun,
And loathsome canker lives in sweetest bud.
All men make faults, and even I in this,
Authorizing thy trespass with compare,
Myself corrupting, salving thy amiss,
Excusing thy sins more than thy sins are;
For to thy sensual fault I bring in sense—
Thy adverse party is thy advocate—
And 'gainst myself a lawful plea commence.
Such civil war is in my love and hate
    That I an accessory needs must be
    To that sweet thief which sourly robs from me.

Let me confess that we two must be twain,
Although our undivided loves are one.
So shall those blots that do with me remain,
Without thy help, by me be borne alone.
In our two loves there is but one respect,
Though in our lives a separable spite,
Which though it alter not love's sole effect,
Yet doth it steal sweet hours from love's delight.
I may not evermore acknowledge thee,
Lest my bewailèd guilt should do thee shame;
Nor thou with public kindness honor me,
Unless thou take that honor from thy name.
　　But do not so; I love thee in such sort
　　As, thou being mine, mine is thy good report.

How can my Muse want subject to invent,
While thou dost breathe, that pour'st into my verse
Thine own sweet argument, too excellent
For every vulgar paper to rehearse?
O, give thyself the thanks, if aught in me
Worthy perusal stand against thy sight;
For who's so dumb that cannot write to thee
When thou thyself dost give invention light?
Be thou the tenth Muse, ten times more in worth
Than those old nine which rhymers invocate;
And he that calls on thee, let him bring forth
Eternal numbers to outlive long date.
    If my slight Muse do please these curious days,
    The pain be mine, but thine shall be the praise.

O, how thy worth with manners may I sing,
When thou art all the better part of me?
What can mine own praise to mine own self bring,
And what is't but mine own when I praise thee?
Even for this, let us divided live,
And our dear love lose name of single one,
That by this separation I may give
That due to thee which thou deserv'st alone.
O, absence, what a torment wouldst thou prove,
Were it not thy sour leisure gave sweet leave
To entertain the time with thoughts of love,
Which time and thoughts so sweetly dost deceive,
    And that thou teachest how to make one twain
    By praising him here who doth hence remain.

Take all my loves, my love, yea take them all;
What hast thou then more than thou hadst before?
No love, my love, that thou mayst true love call;
All mine was thine, before thou hadst this more.
Then if for my love thou my love receivest,
I cannot blame thee for my love thou usest;
But yet be blamed, if thou this self deceivest
By willful taste of what thyself refusest.
I do forgive thy robb'ry, gentle thief,
Although thou steal thee all my poverty;
And yet love knows it is a greater grief
To bear love's wrong than hate's known injury.
    Lascivious grace, in whom all ill well shows,
    Kill me with spites; yet we must not be foes.

Those pretty wrongs that liberty commits,
When I am sometime absent from thy heart,
Thy beauty and thy years full well befits,
For still temptation follows where thou art.
Gentle thou art, and therefore to be won;
Beauteous thou art, therefore to be assailed;
And when a woman woos, what woman's son
Will sourly leave her till she have prevailed?
Ay me, but yet thou might'st my seat forbear,
And chide thy beauty and thy straying youth,
Who lead thee in their riot even there
Where thou art forced to break a twofold truth:
   Hers, by thy beauty tempting her to thee,
   Thine, by thy beauty being false to me.

When most I wink, then do mine eyes best see,
For all the day they view things unrespected,
But when I sleep, in dreams they look on thee
And, darkly bright, are bright in dark directed.
Then thou, whose shadow shadows doth make bright,
How would thy shadow's form form happy show
To the clear day with thy much clearer light,
When to unseeing eyes thy shade shines so!
How would, I say, mine eyes be blessèd made,
By looking on thee in the living day,
When in dead night thy fair imperfect shade
Through heavy sleep on sightless eyes doth stay!
   All days are nights to see till I see thee,
   And nights bright days when dreams do show
      thee me.

If the dull substance of my flesh were thought,
Injurious distance should not stop my way,
For then despite of space I would be brought,
From limits far remote, where thou dost stay.
No matter then although my foot did stand
Upon the farthest earth removed from thee;
For nimble thought can jump both sea and land,
As soon as think the place where he would be.
But, ah, thought kills me that I am not thought,
To leap large lengths of miles when thou art gone,
But that so much of earth and water wrought,
I must attend time's leisure with my moan,
　　Receiving naught by elements so slow
　　But heavy tears, badges of either's woe.

Mine eye and heart are at a mortal war
How to divide the conquest of thy sight;
Mine eye my heart thy picture's sight would bar,
My heart mine eye the freedom of that right.
My heart doth plead that thou in him dost lie—
A closet never pierced with crystal eyes;
But the defendant doth that plea deny,
And says in him thy fair appearance lies.
To 'cide this title is impanelèd
A quest of thoughts, all tenants to the heart;
And by their verdict is determinèd
The clear eye's moiety, and the dear heart's part:
    As thus—mine eye's due is thy outward part,
    And my heart's right thy inward love of heart.

Betwixt mine eye and heart a league is took,
And each doth good turns now unto the other.
When that mine eye is famished for a look,
Or heart in love with sighs himself doth smother,
With my love's picture then my eye doth feast,
And to the painted banquet bids my heart.
Another time mine eye is my heart's guest
And in his thoughts of love doth share a part.
So, either by thy picture or my love,
Thyself away are present still with me;
For thou not farther than my thoughts canst move,
And I am still with them, and they with thee;
    Or, if they sleep, thy picture in my sight
    Awakes my heart to heart's and eye's delight.

How careful was I, when I took my way,
Each trifle under truest bars to thrust,
That to my use it might unusèd stay
From hands of falsehood, in sure wards of trust!
But thou, to whom my jewels trifles are,
Most worthy comfort, now my greatest grief,
Thou best of dearest, and mine only care,
Art left the prey of every vulgar thief.
Thee have I not locked up in any chest,
Save where thou art not, though I feel thou art,
Within the gentle closure of my breast,
From whence at pleasure thou mayst come and part;
   And even thence thou wilt be stol'n, I fear,
   For truth proves thievish for a prize so dear.

Against that time, if ever that time come,
When I shall see thee frown on my defects,
Whenas thy love hath cast his utmost sum,
Called to that audit by advised respects;
Against that time when thou shalt strangely pass,
And scarcely greet me with that sun, thine eye,
When love, converted from the thing it was,
Shall reasons find of settled gravity.
Against that time do I ensconce me here
Within the knowledge of mine own desart,
And this my hand against myself uprear,
To guard the lawful reasons on thy part.
  To leave poor me thou hast the strength of laws,
  Since why to love I can allege no cause.

How heavy do I journey on the way
When what I seek, my weary travel's end,
Doth teach that ease and that repose to say,
"Thus far the miles are measured from thy friend."
The beast that bears me, tired with my woe,
Plods dully on, to bear that weight in me,
As if by some instinct the wretch did know
His rider loved not speed, being made from thee.
The bloody spur cannot provoke him on,
That sometimes anger thrusts into his hide,
Which heavily he answers with a groan,
More sharp to me than spurring to his side;
    For that same groan doth put this in my mind:
    My grief lies onward and my joy behind.

Thus can my love excuse the slow offense
Of my dull bearer, when from thee I speed:
From where thou art why should I haste me thence?
Till I return, of posting is no need.
O, what excuse will my poor beast then find
When swift extremity can seem but slow?
Then should I spur, though mounted on the wind,
In wingèd speed no motion shall I know.
Then can no horse with my desire keep pace;
Therefore desire, of perfect'st love being made,
Shall neigh, no dull flesh in his fiery race;
But love, for love, thus shall excuse my jade:
 Since from thee going he went willful slow,
 Towards thee I'll run and give him leave to go.

So am I as the rich, whose blessèd key
Can bring him to his sweet up-lockèd treasure,
The which he will not ev'ry hour survey,
For blunting the fine point of seldom pleasure.
Therefore are feasts so solemn and so rare,
Since, seldom coming, in the long year set,
Like stones of worth they thinly placèd are,
Or captain jewels in the carcanet.
So is the time that keeps you as my chest,
Or as the wardrobe which the robe doth hide,
To make some special instant special blest,
By new unfolding his imprisoned pride.
　　Blessèd are you whose worthiness gives scope,
　　Being had, to triumph, being lacked, to hope.

What is your substance, whereof are you made,
That millions of strange shadows on you tend?
Since everyone hath, every one, one shade,
And you, but one, can every shadow lend.
Describe Adonis, and the counterfeit
Is poorly imitated after you;
On Helen's cheek all art of beauty set,
And you in Grecian tires are painted new.
Speak of the spring and foison of the year;
The one doth shadow of your beauty show,
The other as your bounty doth appear,
And you in every blessèd shape we know.
    In all external grace you have some part,
    But you like none, none you, for constant heart.

O, how much more doth beauty beauteous seem,
By that sweet ornament which truth doth give!
The rose looks fair, but fairer we it deem
For that sweet odor which doth in it live.
The canker blooms have full as deep a dye,
As the perfumèd tincture of the roses,
Hang on such thorns, and play as wantonly,
When summer's breath their maskèd buds discloses;
But, for their virtue only is their show,
They live unwooed and unrespected fade,
Die to themselves. Sweet roses do not so;
Of their sweet deaths are sweetest odors made.
   And so of you, beauteous and lovely youth,
    When that shall vade, by verse distills your truth.

Not marble, nor the gilded monuments
Of princes, shall outlive this pow'rful rhyme,
But you shall shine more bright in these contents
Than unswept stone, besmeared with sluttish time.
When wasteful war shall statues overturn,
And broils root out the work of masonry,
Nor Mars his sword nor war's quick fire shall burn
The living record of your memory.
'Gainst death and all oblivious enmity
Shall you pace forth; your praise shall still find room
Even in the eyes of all posterity
That wear this world out to the ending doom.
    So, till the judgment that yourself arise,
      You live in this, and dwell in lovers' eyes.

Sweet love, renew thy force; be it not said
Thy edge should blunter be than appetite,
Which but today by feeding is allayed,
Tomorrow sharp'ned in his former might.
So, love, be thou; although today thou fill
Thy hungry eyes even till they wink with fullness,
Tomorrow see again, and do not kill
The spirit of love with a perpetual dullness.
Let this sad int'rim like the ocean be
Which parts the shore where two contracted new
Come daily to the banks, that, when they see
Return of love, more blest may be the view;
    Or call it winter, which being full of care,
    Makes summer's welcome thrice more wished,
      more rare.

Being your slave, what should I do but tend
Upon the hours and times of your desire?
I have no precious time at all to spend,
Nor services to do till you require.
Nor dare I chide the world-without-end hour
Whilst I, my sovereign, watch the clock for you,
Nor think the bitterness of absence sour
When you have bid your servant once adieu.
Nor dare I question with my jealous thought
Where you may be, or your affairs suppose,
But, like a sad slave, stay and think of naught
Save where you are how happy you make those.
    So true a fool is love that in your will,
    Though you do anything, he thinks no ill.

That god forbid that made me first your slave
I should in thought control your times of pleasure,
Or at your hand th' account of hours to crave,
Being your vassal bound to stay your leisure.
O, let me suffer, being at your beck,
Th' imprisoned absence of your liberty;
And patience, tame to sufferance, bide each check,
Without accusing you of injury.
Be where you list, your charter is so strong
That you yourself may privilege your time
To what you will; to you it doth belong
Yourself to pardon of self-doing crime.
   I am to wait, though waiting so be hell,
   Not blame your pleasure, be it ill or well.

Like as the waves make towards the pebbled shore,
So do our minutes hasten to their end;
Each changing place with that which goes before,
In sequent toil all forwards do contend.
Nativity, once in the main of light,
Crawls to maturity, wherewith being crowned,
Crooked eclipses 'gainst his glory fight,
And Time that gave doth now his gift confound.
Time doth transfix the flourish set on youth,
And delves the parallels in beauty's brow,
Feeds on the rarities of nature's truth,
And nothing stands but for his scythe to mow:
    And yet to times in hope my verse shall stand,
    Praising thy worth, despite his cruel hand.

Is it thy will thy image should keep open
My heavy eyelids to the weary night?
Dost thou desire my slumbers should be broken
While shadows like to thee do mock my sight?
Is it thy spirit that thou send'st from thee
So far from home into my deeds to pry,
To find out shames and idle hours in me,
The scope and tenure of thy jealousy?
O no, thy love, though much, is not so great.
It is my love that keeps mine eye awake,
Mine own true love that doth my rest defeat,
To play the watchman ever for thy sake.
  For thee watch I, whilst thou dost wake elsewhere,
  From me far off, with others all too near.

Sin of self-love possesseth all mine eye
And all my soul and all my every part;
And for this sin there is no remedy,
It is so grounded inward in my heart.
Methinks no face so gracious is as mine,
No shape so true, no truth of such account,
And for myself mine own worth do define,
As I all other in all worths surmount.
But when my glass shows me myself indeed,
Beated and chopped with tanned antiquity,
Mine own self-love quite contrary I read;
Self so self-loving were iniquity.
   'Tis thee, myself, that for myself I praise,
   Painting my age with beauty of thy days.

Against my love shall be as I am now,
With Time's injurious hand crushed and o'erworn;
When hours have drained his blood and filled his brow
With lines and wrinkles, when his youthful morn
Hath traveled on to Age's steepy night,
And all those beauties whereof now he's king
Are vanishing, or vanished out of sight,
Stealing away the treasure of his spring;
For such a time do I now fortify
Against confounding Age's cruel knife,
That he shall never cut from memory
My sweet love's beauty, though my lover's life.
  His beauty shall in these black lines be seen,
  And they shall live, and he in them still green.

When I have seen by Time's fell hand defaced
The rich proud cost of outward buried age,
When sometime lofty towers I see down-razed,
And brass eternal slave to mortal rage;
When I have seen the hungry ocean gain
Advantage on the kingdom of the shore,
And the firm soil win of the wat'ry main,
Increasing store with loss and loss with store;
When I have seen such interchange of state,
Or state itself confounded to decay,
Ruin hath taught me thus to ruminate,
That Time will come and take my love away.
   This thought is as a death, which cannot choose
   But weep to have that which it fears to lose.

Since brass, nor stone, nor earth, nor boundless sea,
But sad mortality o'ersways their power,
How with this rage shall beauty hold a plea,
Whose action is no stronger than a flower?
O, how shall summer's honey breath hold out
Against the wrackful siege of batt'ring days,
When rocks impregnable are not so stout,
Nor gates of steel so strong but Time decays?
O, fearful meditation, where, alack,
Shall Time's best jewel from Time's chest lie hid?
Or what strong hand can hold his swift foot back,
Or who his spoil of beauty can forbid?
   O, none, unless this miracle have might,
   That in black ink my love may still shine bright.

Tired with all these, for restful death I cry,
As, to behold desert a beggar born,
And needy nothing trimmed in jollity,
And purest faith unhappily forsworn,
And gilded honor shamefully misplaced,
And maiden virtue rudely strumpeted,
And right perfection wrongfully disgraced,
And strength by limping sway disabled,
And art made tongue-tied by authority,
And folly (doctorlike) controlling skill,
And simple truth miscalled simplicity,
And captive good attending captain ill.
    Tired with all these, from these would I be gone,
    Save that to die, I leave my love alone.

Ah, wherefore with infection should he live,
And with his presence grace impiety,
That sin by him advantage should achieve
And lace itself with his society?
Why should false painting imitate his cheek
And steal dead seeing of his living hue?
Why should poor beauty indirectly seek
Roses of shadow, since his rose is true?
Why should he live, now Nature bankrout is,
Beggared of blood to blush through lively veins,
For she hath no exchequer now but his,
And, proud of many, lives upon his gains?
    O, him she stores, to show what wealth she had,
    In days long since, before these last so bad.

Thus is his cheek the map of days outworn,
When beauty lived and died as flowers do now,
Before these bastard signs of fair were born,
Or durst inhabit on a living brow;
Before the golden tresses of the dead,
The right of sepulchers, were shorn away
To live a second life on second head,
Ere beauty's dead fleece made another gay.
In him those holy antique hours are seen,
Without all ornament, itself and true,
Making no summer of another's green,
Robbing no old to dress his beauty new;
   And him as for a map doth Nature store,
    To show false Art what beauty was of yore.

Those parts of thee that the world's eye doth view
Want nothing that the thought of hearts can mend;
All tongues, the voice of souls, give thee that due,
Utt'ring bare truth, even so as foes commend.
Thy outward thus with outward praise is crowned,
But those same tongues that give thee so thine own
In other accents do this praise confound
By seeing farther than the eye hath shown.
They look into the beauty of thy mind,
And that in guess they measure by thy deeds;
Then, churls, their thoughts, although their eyes
        were kind,
To thy fair flower add the rank smell of weeds;
    But why thy odor matcheth not thy show,
    The soil is this, that thou dost common grow.

That thou art blamed shall not be thy defect,
For slander's mark was ever yet the fair;
The ornament of beauty is suspect,
A crow that flies in heaven's sweetest air.
So thou be good, slander doth but approve
Thy worth the greater, being wooed of time;
For canker vice the sweetest buds doth love,
And thou present'st a pure unstainèd prime.
Thou hast passed by the ambush of young days,
Either not assailed, or victor being charged;
Yet this thy praise cannot be so thy praise
To tie up envy, evermore enlarged.
   If some suspect of ill masked not thy show,
    Then thou alone kingdoms of hearts shouldst owe.

No longer mourn for me when I am dead
Than you shall hear the surly sullen bell
Give warning to the world that I am fled
From this vile world with vilest worms to dwell.
Nay, if you read this line, remember not
The hand that writ it, for I love you so
That I in your sweet thoughts would be forgot,
If thinking on me then should make you woe.
O, if, I say, you look upon this verse,
When I, perhaps, compounded am with clay,
Do not so much as my poor name rehearse,
But let your love even with my life decay,
    Lest the wise world should look into your moan,
    And mock you with me after I am gone.

O, lest the world should task you to recite
What merit lived in me that you should love
After my death, dear love, forget me quite,
For you in me can nothing worthy prove;
Unless you would devise some virtuous lie,
To do more for me than mine own desert,
And hang more praise upon deceasèd I
Than niggard truth would willingly impart.
O, lest your true love may seem false in this,
That you for love speak well of me untrue,
My name be buried where my body is,
And live no more to shame nor me nor you;
    For I am shamed by that which I bring forth,
    And so should you, to love things nothing worth.

That time of year thou mayst in me behold
When yellow leaves, or none, or few, do hang
Upon those boughs which shake against the cold,
Bare ruined choirs where late the sweet birds sang.
In me thou seest the twilight of such day
As after sunset fadeth in the west,
Which by and by black night doth take away,
Death's second self, that seals up all in rest.
In me thou seest the glowing of such fire
That on the ashes of his youth doth lie,
As the deathbed whereon it must expire,
Consumed with that which it was nourished by.
    This thou perceiv'st, which makes thy love
       more strong,
    To love that well which thou must leave ere long.

But be contented. When that fell arrest
Without all bail shall carry me away,
My life hath in this line some interest
Which for memorial still with thee shall stay.
When thou reviewest this, thou dost review
The very part was consecrate to thee.
The earth can have but earth, which is his due;
My spirit is thine, the better part of me.
So then thou hast but lost the dregs of life,
The prey of worms, my body being dead;
The coward conquest of a wretch's knife,
Too base of thee to be rememberèd.
    The worth of that is that which it contains,
    And that is this, and this with thee remains.

So are you to my thoughts as food to life,
Or as sweet-seasoned showers are to the ground;
And for the peace of you I hold such strife
As 'twixt a miser and his wealth is found;
Now proud as an enjoyer, and anon
Doubting the filching age will steal his treasure;
Now counting best to be with you alone,
Then bettered that the world may see my pleasure;
Sometime all full with feasting on your sight,
And by and by clean starvèd for a look;
Possessing or pursuing no delight
Save what is had or must from you be took.
    Thus do I pine and surfeit day by day,
      Or gluttoning on all, or all away.

Why is my verse so barren of new pride,
So far from variation or quick change?
Why with the time do I not glance aside
To new-found methods and to compounds strange?
Why write I still all one, ever the same,
And keep invention in a noted weed,
That every word doth almost tell my name,
Showing their birth, and where they did proceed?
O, know, sweet love, I always write of you,
And you and love are still my argument.
So all my best is dressing all words new,
Spending again what is already spent:
    For as the sun is daily new and old,
    So is my love still telling what is told.

Thy glass will show thee how thy beauties wear,
Thy dial how thy precious minutes waste;
The vacant leaves thy mind's imprint will bear,
And of this book this learning mayst thou taste.
The wrinkles which thy glass will truly show,
Of mouthèd graves, will give thee memory;
Thou by thy dial's shady stealth mayst know
Time's thievish progress to eternity.
Look what thy memory cannot contain,
Commit to these waste blanks, and thou shalt find
Those children nursed, delivered from thy brain,
To take a new acquaintance of thy mind.
　　These offices, so oft as thou wilt look,
　　Shall profit thee, and much enrich thy book.

So oft have I invoked thee for my Muse
And found such fair assistance in my verse
As every alien pen hath got my use
And under thee their poesy disperse.
Thine eyes, that taught the dumb on high to sing
And heavy ignorance aloft to fly,
Have added feathers to the learnèd's wing,
And given grace a double majesty.
Yet be most proud of that which I compile,
Whose influence is thine, and born of thee.
In others' works thou dost but mend the style,
And arts with thy sweet graces gracèd be;
    But thou art all my art and dost advance
    As high as learning my rude ignorance.

Whilst I alone did call upon thy aid,
My verse alone had all thy gentle grace;
But now my gracious numbers are decayed,
And my sick Muse doth give another place.
I grant, sweet love, thy lovely argument
Deserves the travail of a worthier pen,
Yet what of thee thy poet doth invent
He robs thee of, and pays it thee again.
He lends thee virtue, and he stole that word
From thy behavior; beauty doth he give,
And found it in thy cheek; he can afford
No praise to thee but what in thee doth live.
    Then thank him not for that which he doth say,
    Since what he owes thee thou thyself dost pay.

Or I shall live your epitaph to make,
Or you survive when I in earth am rotten.
From hence your memory death cannot take,
Although in me each part will be forgotten.
Your name from hence immortal life shall have,
Though I, once gone, to all the world must die.
The earth can yield me but a common grave,
When you entombèd in men's eyes shall lie.
Your monument shall be my gentle verse,
Which eyes not yet created shall o'erread,
And tongues to be your being shall rehearse
When all the breathers of this world are dead.
    You still shall live—such virtue hath my pen—
    Where breath most breathes, even in the mouths
        of men.

I grant thou wert not married to my Muse,
And therefore mayst without attaint o'erlook
The dedicated words which writers use
Of their fair subject, blessing every book.
Thou art as fair in knowledge as in hue,
Finding thy worth a limit past my praise;
And therefore art enforced to seek anew
Some fresher stamp of the time-bettering days.
And do so, love; yet when they have devised
What strainèd touches rhetoric can lend,
Thou, truly fair, wert truly sympathized
In true plain words by thy true-telling friend:
    And their gross painting might be better used
    Where cheeks need blood; in thee it is abused.

I never saw that you did painting need,
And therefore to your fair no painting set;
I found, or thought I found, you did exceed
The barren tender of a poet's debt;
And therefore have I slept in your report,
That you yourself, being extant, well might show
How far a modern quill doth come too short,
Speaking of worth, what worth in you doth grow.
This silence for my sin you did impute,
Which shall be most my glory, being dumb;
For I impair not beauty, being mute,
When others would give life and bring a tomb.
   There lives more life in one of your fair eyes
   Than both your poets can in praise devise.

Who is it that says most, which can say more
Than this rich praise, that you alone are you,
In whose confine immurèd is the store
Which should example where your equal grew?
Lean penury within that pen doth dwell,
That to his subject lends not some small glory,
But he that writes of you, if he can tell
That you are you, so dignifies his story.
Let him but copy what in you is writ,
Not making worse what nature made so clear,
And such a counterpart shall frame his wit,
Making his style admirèd everywhere.
     You to your beauteous blessings add a curse,
     Being fond on praise, which makes your praises
        worse.

My tongue-tied Muse in manners holds her still
While comments of your praise, richly compiled,
Reserve their character with golden quill
And precious phrase by all the Muses filed.
I think good thoughts whilst other write good words,
And, like unlettered clerk, still cry "Amen"
To every hymn that able spirit affords
In polished form of well-refinèd pen.
Hearing you praised, I say, "'Tis so, 'tis true,"
And to the most of praise add something more;
But that is in my thought, whose love to you,
Though words come hindmost, holds his rank before.
    Then others for the breath of words respect,
    Me for my dumb thoughts, speaking in effect.

Was it the proud full sail of his great verse,
Bound for the prize of all too precious you,
That did my ripe thoughts in my brain inhearse,
Making their tomb the womb wherein they grew?
Was it his spirit, by spirits taught to write
Above a mortal pitch, that struck me dead?
No, neither he, nor his compeers by night
Giving him aid, my verse astonishèd.
He, nor that affable familiar ghost
Which nightly gulls him with intelligence,
As victors, of my silence cannot boast;
I was not sick of any fear from thence.
    But when your countenance filled up his line,
    Then lacked I matter, that enfeebled mine.

Farewell, thou art too dear for my possessing,
And like enough thou know'st thy estimate.
The charter of thy worth gives thee releasing;
My bonds in thee are all determinate.
For how do I hold thee but by thy granting,
And for that riches where is my deserving?
The cause of this fair gift in me is wanting,
And so my patent back again is swerving.
Thyself thou gav'st, thy own worth then not knowing,
Or me, to whom thou gav'st it, else mistaking;
So thy great gift, upon misprision growing,
Comes home again, on better judgment making.
   Thus have I had thee as a dream doth flatter,
   In sleep a king, but waking no such matter.

When thou shalt be disposed to set me light
And place my merit in the eye of scorn,
Upon thy side against myself I'll fight
And prove thee virtuous, though thou art forsworn.
With mine own weakness being best acquainted,
Upon thy part I can set down a story
Of faults concealed wherein I am attainted,
That thou in losing me shall win much glory.
And I by this will be a gainer too,
For, bending all my loving thoughts on thee,
The injuries that to myself I do,
Doing thee vantage, double-vantage me.
   Such is my love, to thee I so belong,
   That for thy right myself will bear all wrong.

Say that thou didst forsake me for some fault,
And I will comment upon that offense.
Speak of my lameness, and I straight will halt,
Against thy reasons making no defense.
Thou canst not, love, disgrace me half so ill,
To set a form upon desirèd change,
As I'll myself disgrace, knowing thy will.
I will acquaintance strangle and look strange;
Be absent from thy walks, and in my tongue
Thy sweet belovèd name no more shall dwell,
Lest I, too much profane, should do it wrong
And haply of our old acquaintance tell.
    For thee, against myself I'll vow debate,
    For I must ne'er love him whom thou dost hate.

Then hate me when thou wilt; if ever, now;
Now, while the world is bent my deeds to cross,
Join with the spite of fortune, make me bow,
And do not drop in for an after-loss.
Ah, do not, when my heart hath 'scaped this sorrow,
Come in the rearward of a conquered woe;
Give not a windy night a rainy morrow,
To linger out a purposed overthrow.
If thou wilt leave me, do not leave me last,
When other petty griefs have done their spite,
But in the onset come; so shall I taste
At first the very worst of fortune's might,
    And other strains of woe, which now seem woe,
    Compared with loss of thee will not seem so.

Some glory in their birth, some in their skill,
Some in their wealth, some in their body's force,
Some in their garments, though newfangled ill,
Some in their hawks and hounds, some in their horse;
And every humor hath his adjunct pleasure,
Wherein it finds a joy above the rest,
But these particulars are not my measure;
All these I better in one general best.
Thy love is better than high birth to me,
Richer than wealth, prouder than garments' cost,
Of more delight than hawks or horses be;
And having thee, of all men's pride I boast:
    Wretched in this alone, that thou mayst take
    All this away, and me most wretched make.

But do thy worst to steal thyself away,
For term of life thou art assurèd mine,
And life no longer than thy love will stay,
For it depends upon that love of thine.
Then need I not to fear the worst of wrongs,
When in the least of them my life hath end.
I see a better state to me belongs
Than that which on thy humor doth depend.
Thou canst not vex me with inconstant mind,
Since that my life on thy revolt doth lie.
O, what a happy title do I find,
Happy to have thy love, happy to die!
    But what's so blessèd-fair that fears no blot?
    Thou mayst be false, and yet I know it not.

So shall I live, supposing thou art true,
Like a deceivèd husband; so love's face
May still seem love to me, though altered new,
Thy looks with me, thy heart in other place.
For there can live no hatred in thine eye;
Therefore in that I cannot know thy change.
In many's looks, the false heart's history
Is writ in moods and frowns and wrinkles strange,
But heaven in thy creation did decree
That in thy face sweet love should ever dwell;
Whate'er thy thoughts or thy heart's workings be,
Thy looks should nothing thence but sweetness tell.
    How like Eve's apple doth thy beauty grow
    If thy sweet virtue answer not thy show.

They that have pow'r to hurt and will do none,
That do not do the thing they most do show,
Who, moving others, are themselves as stone,
Umovèd, cold, and to temptation slow;
They rightly do inherit heaven's graces
And husband nature's riches from expense;
They are the lords and owners of their faces,
Others but stewards of their excellence.
The summer's flow'r is to the summer sweet,
Though to itself it only live and die;
But if that flow'r with base infection meet,
The basest weed outbraves his dignity:
    For sweetest things turn sourest by their deeds;
    Lilies that fester smell far worse than weeds.

How sweet and lovely dost thou make the shame
Which, like a canker in the fragrant rose,
Doth spot the beauty of thy budding name!
O, in what sweets dost thou thy sins enclose!
That tongue that tells the story of thy days,
Making lascivious comments on thy sport,
Cannot dispraise, but in a kind of praise;
Naming thy name blesses an ill report.
O, what a mansion have those vices got
Which for their habitation chose out thee,
Where beauty's veil doth cover every blot,
And all things turns to fair that eyes can see!
   Take heed, dear heart, of this large privilege;
   The hardest knife ill-used doth lose his edge.

Some say thy fault is youth, some wantonness,
Some say thy grace is youth and gentle sport;
Both grace and faults are loved of more and less;
Thou mak'st faults graces that to thee resort.
As on the finger of a thronèd queen
The basest jewel will be well esteemed,
So are those errors that in thee are seen
To truths translated and for true things deemed.
How many lambs might the stern wolf betray,
If like a lamb he could his looks translate;
How many gazers might'st thou lead away,
If thou wouldst use the strength of all thy state!
    But do not so; I love thee in such sort
    As, thou being mine, mine is thy good report.

How like a winter hath my absence been
From thee, the pleasure of the fleeting year!
What freezings have I felt, what dark days seen,
What old December's bareness everywhere!
And yet this time removed was summer's time,
The teeming autumn, big with rich increase,
Bearing the wanton burden of the prime,
Like widowed wombs after their lords' decease.
Yet this abundant issue seemed to me
But hope of orphans and unfathered fruit;
For summer and his pleasures wait on thee,
And, thou away, the very birds are mute;
    Or, if they sing, 'tis with so dull a cheer,
    That leaves look pale, dreading the winter's near.

From you have I been absent in the spring,
When proud-pied April, dressed in all his trim,
Hath put a spirit of youth in everything,
That heavy Saturn laughed and leaped with him,
Yet nor the lays of birds, nor the sweet smell
Of different flowers in odor and in hue,
Could make me any summer's story tell,
Or from their proud lap pluck them where they grew.
Nor did I wonder at the lily's white,
Nor praise the deep vermilion in the rose;
They were but sweet, but figures of delight,
Drawn after you, you pattern of all those.
   Yet seemed it winter still, and, you away,
   As with your shadow I with these did play.

The forward violet thus did I chide:
Sweet thief, whence didst thou steal thy sweet
     that smells
If not from my love's breath? The purple pride
Which on thy soft cheek for complexion dwells
In my love's veins thou hast too grossly dyed.
The lily I condemnèd for thy hand,
And buds of marjoram had stol'n thy hair;
The roses fearfully on thorns did stand,
One blushing shame, another white despair;
A third, nor red nor white, had stol'n of both,
And to his robb'ry had annexed thy breath;
But for his theft, in pride of all his growth
A vengeful canker eat him up to death.
    More flowers I noted, yet I none could see,
    But sweet or color it had stol'n from thee.

Where art thou, Muse, that thou forget'st so long
To speak of that which gives thee all thy might?
Spend'st thou thy fury on some worthless song,
Dark'ning thy pow'r to lend base subjects light?
Return, forgetful Muse, and straight redeem
In gentle numbers time so idly spent,
Sing to the ear that doth thy lays esteem,
And gives thy pen both skill and argument.
Rise, resty Muse, my love's sweet face survey,
If Time have any wrinkle graven there;
If any, be a satire to decay
And make Time's spoils despisèd everywhere.
    Give my love fame faster than Time wastes life;
    So thou prevent'st his scythe and crooked knife.

O truant Muse, what shall be thy amends
For thy negléct of truth in beauty dyed?
Both truth and beauty on my love depends;
So dost thou too, and therein dignified.
Make answer, Muse, wilt thou not haply say,
"Truth needs no color, with his color fixed,
Beauty no pencil, beauty's truth to lay;
But best is best, if never intermixed?"
Because he needs no praise, wilt thou be dumb?
Excuse not silence so, for't lies in thee
To make him much outlive a gilded tomb,
And to be praised of ages yet to be.
   Then do thy office, Muse; I teach thee how
    To make him seem, long hence, as he shows now.

My love is strength'ned, though more weak in
      seeming;
I love not less, though less the show appear.
That love is merchandized whose rich esteeming
The owner's tongue doth publish everywhere.
Our love was new, and then but in the spring,
When I was wont to greet it with my lays,
As Philomel in summer's front doth sing
And stops her pipe in growth of riper days.
Not that the summer is less pleasant now
Than when her mournful hymns did hush the night,
But that wild music burdens every bough,
And sweets grown common lose their dear delight.
    Therefore, like her, I sometime hold my tongue,
    Because I would not dull you with my song.

Alack, what poverty my Muse brings forth,
That, having such a scope to show her pride,
The argument all bare is of more worth
Than when it hath my added praise beside.
O, blame me not if I no more can write!
Look in your glass, and there appears a face
That overgoes my blunt invention quite,
Dulling my lines and doing me disgrace.
Were it not sinful then, striving to mend,
To mar the subject that before was well?
For to no other pass my verses tend
Than of your graces and your gifts to tell;
    And more, much more, than in my verse can sit
    Your own glass shows you when you look in it.

To me, fair friend, you never can be old,
For as you were when first your eye I eyed,
Such seems your beauty still. Three winters cold
Have from the forests shook three summers' pride,
Three beauteous springs to yellow autumn turned
In process of the seasons have I seen,
Three April perfumes in three hot Junes burned,
Since first I saw you fresh, which yet are green.
Ah, yet doth beauty, like a dial hand,
Steal from his figure, and no pace perceived;
So your sweet hue, which methinks still doth stand,
Hath motion, and mine eye may be deceived;
    For fear of which, hear this, thou age unbred:
    Ere you were born was beauty's summer dead.

Let not my love be called idolatry,
Nor my belovèd as an idol show,
Since all alike my songs and praises be
To one, of one, still such, and ever so.
Kind is my love today, tomorrow kind,
Still constant in a wondrous excellence;
Therefore my verse, to constancy confined,
One thing expressing, leaves out difference.
Fair, kind, and true is all my argument,
Fair, kind, and true, varying to other words;
And in this change is my invention spent,
Three themes in one, which wondrous scope affords.
  Fair, kind, and true have often lived alone,
  Which three till now never kept seat in one.

When in the chronicle of wasted time
I see descriptions of the fairest wights,
And beauty making beautiful old rhyme
In praise of ladies dead and lovely knights;
Then, in the blazon of sweet beauty's best,
Of hand, of foot, of lip, of eye, of brow,
I see their antique pen would have expressed
Even such a beauty as you master now.
So all their praises are but prophecies
Of this our time, all you prefiguring,
And, for they looked but with divining eyes,
They had not still enough your worth to sing:
    For we, which now behold these present days,
    Have eyes to wonder, but lack tongues to praise.

Not mine own fears nor the prophetic soul
Of the wide world dreaming on things to come
Can yet the lease of my true love control,
Supposed as forfeit to a confined doom.
The mortal moon hath her eclipse endured,
And the sad augurs mock their own presage,
Incertainties now crown themselves assured,
And peace proclaims olives of endless age.
Now with the drops of this most balmy time
My love looks fresh, and Death to me subscribes,
Since, spite of him, I'll live in this poor rhyme,
While he insults o'er dull and speechless tribes:
    And thou in this shalt find thy monument,
    When tyrants' crests and tombs of brass are spent.

O, never say that I was false of heart,
Though absence seemed my flame to qualify.
As easy might I from myself depart
As from my soul, which in thy breast doth lie.
That is my home of love; if I have ranged,
Like him that travels, I return again,
Just to the time, not with the time exchanged,
So that myself bring water for my stain.
Never believe, though in my nature reigned
All frailties that besiege all kinds of blood,
That it could so preposterously be stained
To leave for nothing all thy sum of good;
    For nothing this wide universe I call
    Save thou, my Rose; in it thou art my all.

Alas, 'tis true I have gone here and there
And made myself a motley to the view,
Gored mine own thoughts, sold cheap what is
        most dear,
Made old offenses of affections new.
Most true it is that I have looked on truth
Askance and strangely; but, by all above,
These blenches gave my heart another youth,
And worse essays proved thee my best of love.
Now all is done, have what shall have no end.
Mine appetite I never more will grind
On newer proof, to try an older friend,
A god in love, to whom I am confined.
    Then give me welcome, next my heaven the best,
    Even to thy pure and most most loving breast.

O, for my sake do you with Fortune chide,
The guilty goddess of my harmful deeds,
That did not better for my life provide
Than public means which public manners breeds.
Thence comes it that my name receives a brand,
And almost thence my nature is subdued
To what it works in, like the dyer's hand.
Pity me then, and wish I were renewed,
Whilst, like a willing patient, I will drink
Potions of eisel 'gainst my strong infection;
No bitterness that I will bitter think,
Nor double penance, to correct correction.
   Pity me then, dear friend, and I assure ye
   Even that your pity is enough to cure me.

Your love and pity doth th' impression fill,
Which vulgar scandal stamped upon my brow;
For what care I who calls me well or ill,
So you o'er-green my bad, my good allow?
You are my all the world, and I must strive
To know my shames and praises from your tongue;
None else to me, nor I to none alive,
That my steeled sense or changes right or wrong.
In so profound abysm I throw all care
Of others' voices, that my adder's sense
To critic and to flatter stoppèd are.
Mark how with my neglect I do dispense:
    You are so strongly in my purpose bred,
    That all the world besides methinks are dead.

Since I left you, mine eye is in my mind,
And that which governs me to go about
Doth part his function and is partly blind,
Seems seeing, but effectually is out;
For it no form delivers to the heart
Of bird, of flow'r, or shape, which it doth latch.
Of his quick objects hath the mind no part,
Nor his own vision holds what it doth catch;
For if it see the rud'st or gentlest sight,
The most sweet favor or deformèd'st creature,
The mountain, or the sea, the day, or night,
The crow, or dove, it shapes them to your feature.
    Incapable of more, replete with you,
    My most true mind thus maketh mine eye untrue.

Or whether doth my mind, being crowned with you,
Drink up the monarch's plague, this flattery?
Or whether shall I say mine eye saith true,
And that your love taught it this alchemy,
To make of monsters, and things indigest,
Such cherubins as your sweet self resemble,
Creating every bad a perfect best
As fast as objects to his beams assemble?
O, 'tis the first, 'tis flatt'ry in my seeing,
And my great mind most kingly drinks it up.
Mine eye well knows what with his gust is 'greeing,
And to his palate doth prepare the cup.
   If it be poisoned, 'tis the lesser sin
    That mine eye loves it and doth first begin.

Those lines that I before have writ do lie,
Even those that said I could not love you dearer.
Yet then my judgment knew no reason why
My most full flame should afterwards burn clearer.
But reckoning Time, whose millioned accidents
Creep in 'twixt vows and change decrees of kings,
Tan sacred beauty, blunt the sharp'st intents,
Divert strong minds to th' course of alt'ring things.
Alas, why, fearing of Time's tyranny,
Might I not then say, "Now I love you best,"
When I was certain o'er incertainty,
Crowning the present, doubting of the rest?
  Love is a babe; then might I not say so,
    To give full growth to that which still doth grow.

Let me not to the marriage of true minds
Admit impediments; love is not love
Which alters when it alteration finds,
Or bends with the remover to remove.
O, no, it is an ever-fixèd mark
That looks on tempests and is never shaken;
It is the star to every wand'ring bark,
Whose worth's unknown, although his height be taken.
Love's not Time's fool, though rosy lips and cheeks
Within his bending sickle's compass come;
Love alters not with his brief hours and weeks,
But bears it out even to the edge of doom.
    If this be error and upon me proved,
    I never writ, nor no man ever loved.

Accuse me thus: that I have scanted all
Wherein I should your great deserts repay,
Forgot upon your dearest love to call,
Whereto all bonds do tie me day by day;
That I have frequent been with unknown minds,
And given to time your own dear-purchased right;
That I have hoisted sail to all the winds
Which should transport me farthest from your sight.
Book both my willfulness and errors down,
And on just proof surmise accumulate;
Bring me within the level of your frown,
But shoot not at me in your wakened hate;
    Since my appeal says I did strive to prove
    The constancy and virtue of your love.

Like as to make our appetites more keen
With eager compounds we our palate urge,
As to prevent our maladies unseen,
We sicken to shun sickness when we purge;
Even so, being full of your ne'er-cloying sweetness,
To bitter sauces did I frame my feeding;
And, sick of welfare, found a kind of meetness
To be diseased ere that there was true needing.
Thus policy in love, t' anticipate
The ills that were not, grew to faults assured,
And brought to medicine a healthful state,
Which, rank of goodness, would by ill be cured.
    But thence I learn, and find the lesson true,
    Drugs poison him that so fell sick of you.

What potions have I drunk of Siren tears
Distilled from limbecks foul as hell within,
Applying fears to hopes and hopes to fears,
Still losing when I saw myself to win!
What wretched errors hath my heart committed,
Whilst it hath thought itself so blessèd never!
How have mine eyes out of their spheres been fitted
In the distraction of this madding fever!
O, benefit of ill: now I find true
That better is by evil still made better;
And ruined love, when it is built anew,
Grows fairer than at first, more strong, far greater.
   So I return rebuked to my content,
    And gain by ills thrice more than I have spent.

That you were once unkind befriends me now,
And for that sorrow which I then did feel
Needs must I under my transgression bow,
Unless my nerves were brass or hammered steel.
For if you were by my unkindness shaken,
As I by yours, y'have passed a hell of time,
And I, a tyrant, have no leisure taken
To weigh how once I suffered in your crime.
O, that our night of woe might have rememb'red
My deepest sense how hard true sorrow hits,
And soon to you, as you to me then, tend'red
The humble salve which wounded bosoms fits!
   But that your trespass now becomes a fee;
   Mine ransoms yours, and yours must ransom me.

'Tis better to be vile than vile esteemed
When not to be receives reproach of being,
And the just pleasure lost, which is so deemed
Not by our feeling, but by others' seeing.
For why should others' false adulterate eyes
Give salutation to my sportive blood?
Or on my frailties why are frailer spies,
Which in their wills count bad what I think good?
No, I am that I am, and they that level
At my abuses reckon up their own;
I may be straight though they themselves be bevel.
By their rank thoughts my deeds must not be shown,
    Unless this general evil they maintain:
    All men are bad and in their badness reign.

No, Time, thou shalt not boast that I do change.
Thy pyramids built up with newer might
To me are nothing novel, nothing strange;
They are but dressings of a former sight.
Our dates are brief, and therefore we admire
What thou dost foist upon us that is old,
And rather make them born to our desire
Than think that we before have heard them told.
Thy registers and thee I both defy,
Not wond'ring at the present, nor the past;
For thy records and what we see doth lie,
Made more or less by thy continual haste.
    This I do vow, and this shall ever be:
    I will be true despite thy scythe and thee.

If my dear love were but the child of state,
It might for Fortune's bastard be unfathered,
As subject to Time's love, or to Time's hate,
Weeds among weeds, or flowers with flowers gathered.
No, it was builded far from accident;
It suffers not in smiling pomp, nor falls
Under the blow of thrallèd discontent,
Whereto th' inviting time our fashion calls.
It fears not Policy, that heretic,
Which works on leases of short-numb'red hours,
But all alone stands hugely politic,
That it nor grows with heat, nor drowns with showers.
   To this I witness call the fools of Time,
    Which die for goodness, who have lived for crime.

O thou, my lovely boy, who in thy power
Dost hold Time's fickle glass, his sickle hour,
Who hast by waning grown, and therein show'st
Thy lovers withering, as thy sweet self grow'st;
If Nature, sovereign mistress over wrack,
As thou goest onwards, still will pluck thee back,
She keeps thee to this purpose, that her skill
May Time disgrace and wretched minutes kill.
Yet fear her, O thou minion of her pleasure;
She may detain, but not still keep her treasure.
   Her audit, though delayed, answered must be,
    And her quietus is to render thee.

In the old age black was not counted fair,
Or, if it were, it bore not beauty's name.
But now is black beauty's successive heir,
And beauty slandered with a bastard shame;
For since each hand hath put on nature's power,
Fairing the foul with art's false borrowed face,
Sweet beauty hath no name, no holy bower,
But is profaned, if not lives in disgrace.
Therefore my mistress' eyes are raven black,
Her eyes so suited, and they mourners seem,
At such who, not born fair, no beauty lack,
Sland'ring creation with a false esteem:
    Yet so they mourn, becoming of their woe,
      That every tongue says beauty should look so.

How oft, when thou, my music, music play'st
Upon that bléssèd wood whose motion sounds
With thy sweet fingers when thou gently sway'st
The wiry concord that mine ear confounds,
Do I envy those jacks that nimble leap
To kiss the tender inward of thy hand,
Whilst my poor lips, which should that harvest reap,
At the wood's boldness by thee blushing stand.
To be so tickled, they would change their state
And situation with those dancing chips
O'er whom thy fingers walk with gentle gait,
Making dead wood more blest than living lips.
    Since saucy jacks so happy are in this,
    Give them thy fingers, me thy lips to kiss.

Th' expense of spirit in a waste of shame
Is lust in action; and, till action, lust
Is perjured, murd'rous, bloody, full of blame,
Savage, extreme, rude, cruel, not to trust;
Enjoyed no sooner but despisèd straight;
Past reason hunted, and no sooner had,
Past reason hated as a swallowed bait
On purpose laid to make the taker mad;
Made in pursuit, and in possession so;
Had, having, and in quest to have, extreme;
A bliss in proof, and proved, a very woe,
Before, a joy proposed; behind, a dream.
    All this the world well knows, yet none knows well
    To shun the heaven that leads men to this hell.

My mistress' eyes are nothing like the sun;
Coral is far more red than her lips' red;
If snow be white, why then her breasts are dun;
If hairs be wires, black wires grown on her head.
I have seen roses damasked, red and white,
But no such roses see I in her cheeks,
And in some perfumes is there more delight
Than in the breath that from my mistress reeks.
I love to hear her speak, yet well I know
That music hath a far more pleasing sound.
I grant I never saw a goddess go;
My mistress when she walks treads on the ground.
   And yet, by heaven, I think my love as rare
   As any she belied with false compare.

Thou art as tyrannous, so as thou art,
As those whose beauties proudly make them cruel;
For well thou know'st to my dear doting heart
Thou art the fairest and most precious jewel.
Yet, in good faith, some say that thee behold,
Thy face hath not the power to make love groan;
To say they err I dare not be so bold,
Although I swear it to myself alone.
And, to be sure that is not false I swear,
A thousand groans, but thinking on thy face,
One on another's neck, do witness bear
Thy black is fairest in my judgment's place.
   In nothing art thou black save in thy deeds,
   And thence this slander, as I think, proceeds.

Thine eyes I love, and they, as pitying me,
Knowing thy heart torment me with disdain,
Have put on black and loving mourners be,
Looking with pretty ruth upon my pain.
And truly not the morning sun of heaven
Better becomes the gray cheeks of the east,
Nor that full star that ushers in the even
Doth half that glory to the sober west
As those two mourning eyes become thy face.
O, let it then as well beseem thy heart
To mourn for me, since mourning doth thee grace,
And suit thy pity like in every part.
    Then will I swear beauty herself is black,
    And all they foul that thy complexion lack.

Beshrew that heart that makes my heart to groan
For that deep wound it gives my friend and me.
Is't not enough to torture me alone,
But slave to slavery my sweet'st friend must be?
Me from myself thy cruel eye hath taken,
And my next self thou harder hast engrossed.
Of him, myself, and thee, I am forsaken;
A torment thrice threefold thus to be crossed.
Prison my heart in thy steel bosom's ward,
But then my friend's heart let my poor heart bail;
Whoe'er keeps me, let my heart be his guard;
Thou canst not then use rigor in my jail.
   And yet thou wilt, for I, being pent in thee,
   Perforce am thine, and all that is in me.

Whoever hath her wish, thou hast thy *Will*,
And *Will* to boot, and *Will* in overplus;
More than enough am I that vex thee still,
To thy sweet will making addition thus.
Wilt thou, whose will is large and spacious,
Not once vouchsafe to hide my will in thine?
Shall will in others seem right gracious,
And in my will no fair acceptance shine?
The sea, all water, yet receives rain still
And in abundance addeth to his store;
So thou being rich in *Will* add to thy *Will*
One will of mine, to make thy large *Will* more.
    Let no unkind, no fair beseechers kill;
    Think all but one, and me in that one *Will*.

When my love swears that she is made of truth,
I do believe her though I know she lies,
That she might think me some untutored youth,
Unlearnèd in the world's false subtleties.
Thus vainly thinking that she thinks me young,
Although she knows my days are past the best,
Simply I credit her false-speaking tongue;
On both sides thus is simple truth suppressed.
But wherefore says she not she is unjust?
And wherefore say not I that I am old?
O, love's best habit is in seeming trust,
And age in love loves not to have years told.
    Therefore I lie with her, and she with me,
    And in our faults by lies we flattered be.

Be wise as thou art cruel; do not press
My tongue-tied patience with too much disdain,
Lest sorrow lend me words, and words express
The manner of my pity-wanting pain.
If I might teach thee wit, better it were,
Though not to love, yet love, to tell me so;
As testy sick men, when their deaths be near,
No news but health from their physicians know.
For if I should despair, I should grow mad,
And in my madness might speak ill of thee.
Now this ill-wresting world is grown so bad
Mad slanderers by mad ears believèd be.
　　That I may not be so, nor thou belied,
　　Bear thine eyes straight, though thy proud heart
　　　go wide.

In faith I do not love thee with mine eyes,
For they in thee a thousand errors note;
But 'tis my heart that loves what they despise,
Who in despite of view is pleased to dote.
Nor are mine ears with thy tongue's tune delighted,
Nor tender feeling to base touches prone,
Nor taste, nor smell, desire to be invited
To any sensual feast with thee alone.
But my five wits nor my five senses can
Dissuade one foolish heart from serving thee,
Who leaves unswayed the likeness of a man,
Thy proud heart's slave and vassal wretch to be.
   Only my plague thus far I count my gain,
    That she that makes me sin awards me pain.

Love is my sin, and thy dear virtue hate,
Hate of my sin, grounded on sinful loving.
O, but with mine compare thou thine own state,
And thou shalt find it merits not reproving,
Of if it do, not from those lips of thine,
That have profaned their scarlet ornaments
And sealed false bonds of love as oft as mine,
Robbed others' beds' revenues of their rents.
Be it lawful I love thee as thou lov'st those
Whom thine eyes woo as mine importune thee.
Root pity in thy heart, that, when it grows,
Thy pity may deserve to pitied be.
　　If thou dost seek to have what thou dost hide,
　　By self-example mayst thou be denied.

Two loves I have, of comfort and despair,
Which like two spirits do suggest me still;
The better angel is a man right fair,
The worser spirit a woman colored ill.
To win me soon to hell, my female evil
Tempteth my better angel from my side,
And would corrupt my saint to be a devil,
Wooing his purity with her foul pride.
And whether that my angel be turned fiend
Suspect I may, yet not directly tell;
But being both from me, both to each friend,
I guess one angel in another's hell.
    Yet this shall I ne'er know, but live in doubt,
    Till my bad angel fire my good one out.

Those lips that Love's own hand did make
Breathed forth the sound that said, "I hate"
To me that languished for her sake.
But when she saw my woeful state,
Straight in her heart did mercy come,
Chiding that tongue that ever sweet
Was used in giving gentle doom,
And taught it thus anew to greet:
"I hate," she altered with an end
That followed it as gentle day
Doth follow night, who, like a fiend,
From heaven to hell is flown away.
　　"I hate" from hate away she threw,
　　And saved my life, saying, "not you."

Poor soul, the center of my sinful earth,
My sinful earth these rebel pow'rs that thee array,
Why dost thou pine within and suffer dearth,
Painting thy outward walls so costly gay?
Why so large cost, having so short a lease,
Dost thou upon thy fading mansion spend?
Shall worms, inheritors of this excess,
Eat up thy charge? Is this thy body's end?
Then, soul, live thou upon thy servant's loss,
And let that pine to aggravate thy store;
Buy terms divine in selling hours of dross;
Within be fed, without be rich no more:
   So shalt thou feed on Death, that feeds on men,
    And Death once dead, there's no more dying then.

My love is as a fever, longing still
For that which longer nurseth the disease,
Feeding on that which doth preserve the ill,
Th' uncertain sickly appetite to please.
My reason, the physician to my love,
Angry that his prescriptions are not kept,
Hath left me, and I desperate now approve
Desire is death, which physic did except.
Past cure I am, now reason is past care,
And frantic-mad with evermore unrest;
My thoughts and my discourse as madmen's are,
At random from the truth vainly expressed:
    For I have sworn thee fair, and thought thee bright,
    Who art as black as hell, as dark as night.

Canst thou, O cruel, say I love thee not,
When I against myself with thee partake?
Do I not think on thee when I forgot
Am of myself, all tyrant for thy sake?
Who hateth thee that I do call my friend?
On whom frown'st thou that I do fawn upon?
Nay, if thou lour'st on me, do I not spend
Revenge upon myself with present moan?
What merit do I in myself respect
That is so proud thy service to despise,
When all my best doth worship thy defect,
Commanded by the motion of thine eyes?
   But, love, hate on, for now I know thy mind;
    Those that can see thou lov'st, and I am blind.

Love is too young to know what conscience is,
Yet who knows not conscience is born of love?
Then, gentle cheater, urge not my amiss,
Lest guilty of my faults thy sweet self prove.
For, thou betraying me, I do betray
My nobler part to my gross body's treason;
My soul doth tell my body that he may
Triumph in love; flesh stays no farther reason,
But, rising at thy name, doth point out thee,
As his triumphant prize. Proud of this pride,
He is contented thy poor drudge to be,
To stand in thy affairs, fall by thy side.
    No want of conscience hold it that I call
    Her "love" for whose dear love I rise and fall.

In loving thee thou know'st I am forsworn,
But thou art twice forsworn, to me love swearing;
In act thy bed-vow broke, and new faith torn
In vowing new hate after new love bearing.
But why of two oaths' breach do I accuse thee,
When I break twenty? I am perjured most,
For all my vows are oaths but to misuse thee,
And all my honest faith in thee is lost;
For I have sworn deep oaths of thy deep kindness,
Oaths of thy love, thy truth, thy constancy;
And, to enlighten thee, gave eyes to blindness,
Or made them swear against the thing they see;
    For I have sworn thee fair; more perjured eye,
      To swear against the truth so foul a lie.

Cupid laid by his brand and fell asleep.
A maid of Dián's this advantage found,
And his love-kindling fire did quickly steep
In a cold valley-fountain of that ground;
Which borrowed from this holy fire of Love
A dateless lively heat, still to endure,
And grew a seething bath, which yet men prove
Against strange maladies a sovereign cure.
But at my mistress' eye Love's brand new-fired,
The boy for trial needs would touch my breast;
I, sick withal, the help of bath desired,
And thither hied, a sad distempered guest,
    But found no cure; the bath for my help lies
    Where Cupid got new fire—my mistress' eyes.

NARRATIVE
POEMS

From VENUS AND ADONIS

Even as an empty eagle, sharp by fast,
Tires with her beak on feathers, flesh, and bone,
Shaking her wings, devouring all in haste,
Till either gorge be stuffed or prey be gone—
 Even so she kissed his brow, his cheek, his chin,
 And where she ends she doth anew begin.

Forced to content, but never to obey,
Panting he lies and breatheth in her face.
She feedeth on the steam as on a prey
And calls it heavenly moisture, air of grace,
 Wishing her cheeks were gardens full of flowers,
 So they were dewed with such distilling showers.

Look how a bird lies tangled in a net,
So fastened in her arms Adonis lies.
Pure shame and awed resistance made him fret,
Which bred more beauty in his angry eyes:
 Rain added to a river that is rank
 Perforce will force it overflow the bank.

Still she entreats, and prettily entreats,
For to a pretty ear she tunes her tale.
Still is he sullen, still he low'rs and frets,
'Twixt crimson shame and anger ashy-pale.
    Being red, she loves him best; and being white,
    Her best is bettered with a more delight.

Look how he can, she cannot choose but love;
And by her fair immortal hand she swears
From his soft bosom never to remove
Till he take truce with her contending tears,
    Which long have rained, making her cheeks all wet;
    And one sweet kiss shall pay this comptless debt.

* * * * *

"Bid me discourse, I will enchant thine ear,
Or like a fairy trip upon the green,
Or like a nymph with long dishevelled hair,
Dance on the sands, and yet no footing seen.
    Love is a spirit all compact of fire,
    Not gross to sink, but light, and will aspire.

"Witness this primrose bank whereon I lie;
These forceless flowers like sturdy trees support me.
Two strengthless doves will draw me through the sky
From morn till night, even where I list to sport me.
    Is love so light, sweet boy, and may it be
    That thou should think it heavy unto thee?

"Is thine own heart to thine own face affected?
Can thy right hand seize love upon thy left?
Then woo thyself, be of thyself rejected;
Steal thine own freedom, and complain on theft.
    Narcissus so himself himself forsook,
    And died to kiss his shadow in the brook.

"Torches are made to light, jewels to wear,
Dainties to taste, fresh beauty for the use,
Herbs for their smell, and sappy plants to bear.
Things growing to themselves are growth's abuse.
    Seeds spring from seeds, and beauty breedeth
        beauty.
    Thou wast begot; to get it is thy duty.

"Upon the earth's increase why shouldst thou feed
Unless the earth with thy increase be fed?
By law of nature thou art bound to breed,
That thine may live when thou thyself art dead;
   And so in spite of death thou dost survive,
   In that thy likeness still is left alive."

     *   *   *   *   *

He sees her coming and begins to glow,
Even as a dying coal revives with wind,
And with his bonnet hides his angry brow,
Looks on the dull earth with disturbèd mind,
   Taking no notice that she is so nigh,
   For all askance he holds her in his eye.

O, what a sight it was, wistly to view
How she came stealing to the wayward boy!
To note the fighting conflict of her hue,
How white and red each other did destroy!
   But now her cheek was pale, and by and by
   It flashed forth fire, as lightning from the sky.

Now was she just before him as he sat,
And like a lowly lover down she kneels;
With one fair hand she heaveth up his hat,
Her other tender hand his fair cheek feels.
  His tend'rer cheek receives her soft hand's print
  As apt as new-fall'n snow takes any dint.

* * * * *

Her song was tedious and outwore the night,
For lovers' hours are long, though seeming short.
If pleased themselves, others, they think, delight
In such-like circumstance, with such-like sport.
  Their copious stories, oftentimes begun,
  End without audience, and are never done.

For who hath she to spend the night withal
But idle sounds resembling parasits,
Like shrill-tongued tapsters answering every call,
Soothing the humor of fantastic wits?
  She says "'Tis so." They answer all, "'Tis so,"
  And would say after her if she said "No."

Lo, here the gentle lark, weary of rest,
From his moist cabinet mounts up on high
And wakes the morning, from whose silver breast
The sun ariseth in his majesty;
    Who doth the world so gloriously behold
    That cedar tops and hills seem burnished gold.

Venus salutes him with this fair good-morrow:
"O thou clear god, and patron of all light,
From whom each lamp and shining star doth borrow
The beauteous influence that makes him bright;
    There lives a son that sucked an earthly mother
    May lend thee light, as thou dost lend to other."

This said, she hasteth to a myrtle grove,
Musing the morning is so much o'erworn
And yet she hears no tidings of her love.
She hearkens for his hounds and for his horn.
    Anon she hears them chant it lustily,
    And all in haste she coasteth to the cry.

*   *   *   *   *

By this the boy that by her side lay killed
Was melted like a vapor from her sight,
And in his blood, that on the ground lay spilled,
A purple flower sprung up, check'red with white,
    Resembling well his pale cheeks and the blood
    Which in round drops upon their whiteness stood.

She bows her head the new-sprung flower to smell,
Comparing it to her Adonis' breath,
And says within her bosom it shall dwell,
Since he himself is reft from her by death;
    She crops the stalk, and in the breach appears
    Green-dropping sap, which she compares to tears.

"Poor flow'r," quoth she, "this was thy father's guise—
Sweet issue of a more sweet-smelling sire—
For every little grief to wet his eyes;
To grow unto himself was his desire,
    And so 'tis thine; but know, it is as good
    To wither in my breast as in his blood.

"Here was thy father's bed, here in my breast;
Thou art the next of blood, and 'tis thy right.
Lo in this hollow cradle take thy rest;
My throbbing heart shall rock thee day and night:
    There shall not be one minute in an hour
    Wherein I will not kiss my sweet love's flow'r."

Thus weary of the world, away she hies,
And yokes her silver doves, by whose swift aid
Their mistress, mounted, though the empty skies
In her light chariot quickly is conveyed,
    Holding their course to Paphos, where their queen
    Means to immure herself and not be seen.

FINIS

From THE RAPE OF LUCRECE

Into the chamber wickedly he stalks
And gazeth on her yet unstainèd bed.
The curtains being close, about he walks,
Rolling his greedy eyeballs in his head.
By their high treason is his heart misled,
    Which gives the watchword to his hand full soon
    To draw the cloud that hides the silver moon.

Look as the fair and fiery-pointed sun,
Rushing from forth a cloud, bereaves our sight,
Even so, the curtain drawn, his eyes begun
To wink, being blinded with a greater light.
Whether it is that she reflects so bright
    That dazzleth them, or else some shame supposèd;
    But blind they are, and keep themselves enclosèd.

O, had they in that darksome prison died,
Then had they seen the period of their ill!
Then Collatine again by Lucrece' side
In his clear bed might have reposèd still.
But they must ope, this blessèd league to kill,
    And holy-thoughted Lucrece to their sight
    Must sell her joy, her life, her world's delight.

Her lily hand her rosy cheek lies under,
Coz'ning the pillow of a lawful kiss;
Who, therefore angry, seems to part in sunder,
Swelling on either side to want his bliss;
Between whose hills her head entombèd is;
    Where like a virtuous monument she lies,
    To be admired of lewd unhallowed eyes.

Without the bed her other fair hand was,
On the green coverlet; whose perfect white
Showed like an April daisy on the grass,
With pearly sweat resembling dew of night.
Her eyes like marigolds had sheathed their light,
    And canopied in darkness sweetly lay
    Till they might open to adorn the day.

Her hair like golden threads played with her breath—
O modest wantons, wanton modesty—
Showing life's triumph in the map of death,
And death's dim look in life's mortality.
Each in her sleep themselves so beautify
    As if between them twain there were no strife,
    But that life lived in death, and death in life.

Her breasts like ivory globes circled with blue,
A pair of maiden worlds unconquerèd,
Save of their lord no bearing yoke they knew,
And him by oath they truly honorèd.
These worlds in Tarquin new ambition bred,
    Who like a foul usurper went about
    From this fair throne to heave the owner out.

What could he see but mightily he noted?
What did he note but strongly he desirèd?
What he beheld, on that he firmly doted,
And in his will his willful eye he tirèd.
With more than admiration he admirèd
    Her azure veins, her alablaster skin,
    Her coral lips, her snow-white dimpled chin.

As the grim lion fawneth o'er his prey,
Sharp hunger by the conquest satisfied,
So o'er this sleeping soul doth Tarquin stay,
His rage of lust by gazing qualified;
Slacked, not suppressed; for, standing by her side,
    His eye, which late this mutiny restrains,
    Unto a greater uproar tempts his veins.

And they, like straggling slaves for pillage fighting,
Obdurate vassals fell exploits effecting,
In bloody death and ravishment delighting,
Nor children's tears nor mothers' groans respecting,
Swell in their pride, the onset still expecting.
  Anon his beating heart, alarum striking,
  Gives the hot charge and bids them do their liking.

His drumming heart cheers up his burning eye,
His eye commends the leading to his hand;
His hand, as proud of such a dignity,
Smoking with pride, marched on to make his stand
On her bare breast, the heart of all her land;
  Whose ranks of blue veins, as his hand did scale,
  Left their round turrets destitute and pale.

They, must'ring to the quiet cabinet
Where their dear governess and lady lies,
Do tell her she is dreadfully beset
And fright her with confusion of their cries.
She, much amazed, breaks ope her locked-up eyes,
  Who, peeping forth this tumult to behold,
  Are by his flaming torch dimmed and controlled.

Imagine her as one in dead of night,
From forth dull sleep by dreadful fancy waking,
That thinks she hath beheld some ghastly sprite,
Whose grim aspect sets every joint a-shaking.
What terror 'tis! but she, in worser taking,
    From sleep disturbèd, heedfully doth view
    The sight which makes supposèd terror true.

Wrapped and confounded in a thousand fears,
Like to a new-killed bird she trembling lies.
She dares not look; yet winking there appears
Quick-shifting antics, ugly in her eyes.
Such shadows are the weak brain's forgeries,
    Who, angry that the eyes fly from their lights,
    In darkness daunts them with more dreadful sights.

His hand, that yet remains upon her breast
(Rude ram, to batter such an ivory wall),
May feel her heart (poor citizen) distressed,
Wounding itself to death, rise up and fall,
Beating her bulk, that his hand shakes withal.
    This moves in him more rage and lesser pity,
    To make the breach and enter this sweet city.

First like a trumpet doth his tongue begin
To sound a parley to his heartless foe;
Who o'er the white sheet peers her whiter chin,
The reason of this rash alarm to know,
Which he by dumb demeanor seeks to show;
　　But she with vehement prayers urgeth still
　　Under what color he commits this ill.

Thus he replies: "The color in thy face,
That even for anger makes the lily pale
And the red rose blush at her own disgrace,
Shall plead for me and tell my loving tale.
Under that color am I come to scale
　　Thy never-conquered fort; the fault is thine,
　　For those thine eyes betray thee unto mine.

"Thus I forestall thee, if thou mean to chide:
Thy beauty hath ensnared thee to this night,
Where thou with patience must my will abide,
My will that marks thee for my earth's delight,
Which I to conquer sought with all my might;
　　But as reproof and reason beat it dead,
　　By thy bright beauty was it newly bred.

"I see what crosses my attempt will bring,
I know what thorns the growing rose defends,
I think the honey guarded with a sting:
All this beforehand counsel comprehends.
But Will is deaf, and hears no heedful friends;
   Only he hath an eye to gaze on Beauty,
   And dotes on what he looks, 'gainst law or duty.

"I have debated even in my soul,
What wrong, what shame, what sorrow I shall breed;
But nothing can affection's course control
Or stop the headlong fury of his speed.
I know repentant tears ensue the deed,
   Reproach, disdain, and deadly enmity;
   Yet strive I to embrace mine infamy."

This said, he shakes aloft his Roman blade,
Which, like a falcon tow'ring in the skies,
Coucheth the fowl below with his wings' shade,
Whose crooked beak threats if he mount he dies.
So under his insulting falchion lies
   Harmless Lucretia, marking what he tells
   With trembling fear, as fowl hear falcons' bells.

"Lucrece," quoth he, "this night I must enjoy thee.
If thou deny, then force must work my way;
For in thy bed I purpose to destroy thee.
That done, some worthless slave of thine I'll slay,
To kill thine honor with thy life's decay;
  And in thy dead arms do I mean to place him,
  Swearing I slew him, seeing thee embrace him.

"So thy surviving husband shall remain
The scornful mark of every open eye;
Thy kinsmen hang their heads at this disdain,
Thy issue blurred with nameless bastardy;
And thou, the author of their obloquy,
  Shalt have thy trespass cited up in rhymes
  And sung by children in succeeding times.

"But if thou yield, I rest thy secret friend;
The fault unknown is as a thought unacted.
A little harm done to a great good end
For lawful policy remains enacted.
The poisonous simple sometime is compacted
  In a pure compound; being so applied,
  His venom in effect is purified.

"Then, for thy husband and thy children's sake,
Tender my suit; bequeath not to their lot
The shame that from them no device can take,
The blemish that will never be forgot;
Worse than a slavish wipe or birth-hour's blot;
    For marks descried in men's nativity
    Are nature's faults, not their own infamy."

Here with a cockatrice' dead-killing eye
He rouseth up himself and makes a pause;
While she, the picture of pure piety,
Like a white hind under the gripe's sharp claws,
Pleads, in a wilderness where are no laws,
    To the rough beast that knows no gentle right
    Nor aught obeys but his foul appetite.

But when a black-faced cloud the world doth threat,
In his dim mist th' aspiring mountains hiding,
From earth's dark womb some gentle gust doth get,
Which blows these pitchy vapors from their biding,
Hind'ring their present fall by this dividing,
    So his unhallowed haste her words delays,
    And moody Pluto winks while Orpheus plays.

Yet, foul night-waking cat, he doth but dally,
While in his hold-fast foot the weak mouse panteth.
Her sad behavior feeds his vulture folly,
A swallowing gulf that even in plenty wanteth.
His ear her prayers admits, but his heart granteth
   No penetrable entrance to her plaining.
   Tears harden lust, though marble wear with raining.

Her pity-pleading eyes are sadly fixèd
In the remorseless wrinkles of his face.
Her modest eloquence with sighs is mixèd,
Which to her oratory adds more grace.
She puts the period often from his place,
   And midst the sentence so her accent breaks
   That twice she doth begin ere once she speaks.

She conjures him by high almighty Jove,
By knighthood, gentry, and sweet friendship's oath,
By her untimely tears, her husband's love,
By holy human law and common troth,
By heaven and earth, and all the power of both,
   That to his borrowed bed he make retire
   And stoop to honor, not to foul desire.

Quoth she, "Reward not hospitality
With such black payment as thou hast pretended;
Mud not the fountain that gave drink to thee;
Mar not the thing that cannot be amended.
End thy ill aim before thy shoot be ended.
　　He is no woodman that doth bend his bow
　　To strike a poor unseasonable doe.

"My husband is thy friend; for his sake spare me.
Thyself art mighty; for thine own sake leave me.
Myself a weakling; do not then ensnare me.
Thou look'st not like deceit; do not deceive me.
My sighs like whirlwinds labor hence to heave thee.
　　If ever man were moved with woman's moans,
　　Be movèd with my tears, my sighs, my groans;

"All which together, like a troubled ocean,
Beat at thy rocky and wrack-threat'ning heart,
To soften it with their continual motion;
For stones dissolved to water do convert.
O, if no harder than a stone thou art,
　　Melt at my tears and be compassionate!
　　Soft pity enters at an iron gate.

"In Tarquin's likeness I did entertain thee;
Hast thou put on his shape to do him shame?
To all the host of heaven I complain me.
Thou wrong'st his honor, wound'st his princely name.
Thou art not what thou seem'st; and if the same,
    Thou seem'st not what thou art, a god, a king;
    For kings like gods should govern everything.

"How will thy shame be seeded in thine age
When thus thy vices bud before thy spring?
If in thy hope thou dar'st do such outrage,
What dar'st thou not when once thou art a king?
O, be rememb'red, no outrageous thing
    From vassal actors can be wiped away;
    Then kings' misdeeds cannot be hid in clay.

"This deed will make thee only loved for fear;
But happy monarchs still are feared for love.
With foul offenders thou perforce must bear
When they in thee the like offenses prove.
If but for fear of this, thy will remove;
    For princes are the glass, the school, the book,
    Where subjects' eyes do learn, do read, do look."

*   *   *   *   *

This said, he sets his foot upon the light,
For light and lust are deadly enemies;
Shame folded up in blind concealing night,
When most unseen, then most doth tyrannize.
The wolf hath seized his prey; the poor lamb cries,
　　Till with her own white fleece her voice controlled
　　Entombs her outcry in her lips' sweet fold;

For with the nightly linen that she wears
He pens her piteous clamors in her head,
Cooling his hot face in the chastest tears
That ever modest eyes with sorrow shed.
O, that prone lust should stain so pure a bed,
　　The spots whereof, could weeping purify,
　　Her tears should drop on them perpetually!

But she hath lost a dearer thing than life,
And he hath won what he would lose again.
This forcèd league doth force a further strife;
This momentary joy breeds months of pain;
This hot desire converts to cold disdain;
　　Pure Chastity is rifled of her store,
　　And Lust, the thief, far poorer than before.

Look as the full-fed hound or gorgèd hawk,
Unapt for tender smell or speedy flight,
Make slow pursuit, or altogether balk
The prey wherein by nature they delight,
So surfeit-taking Tarquin fares this night:
    His taste delicious, in digestion souring,
    Devours his will, that lived by foul devouring.

*   *   *   *   *

O, deeper sin than bottomless conceit
Can comprehend in still imagination!
Drunken Desire must vomit his receipt
Ere he can see his own abomination.
While Lust is in his pride, no exclamation
    Can curb his heat or rein his rash desire
    Till, like a jade, Self-will himself doth tire.

And then with lank and lean discolored cheek,
With heavy eye, knit brow, and strengthless pace,
Feeble Desire, all recreant, poor, and meek,
Like to a bankrout beggar wails his case.
The flesh being proud, Desire doth fight with Grace,
    For there it revels; and when that decays,
    The guilty rebel for remission prays.

So fares it with this fault-full lord of Rome,
Who this accomplishment so hotly chasèd;
For now against himself he sounds this doom,
That through the length of times he stands disgracèd.
Besides, his soul's fair temple is defacèd;
  To whose weak ruins muster troops of cares,
  To ask the spotted princess how she fares.

She says her subjects with foul insurrection
Have battered down her consecrated wall,
And by their mortal fault brought in subjection
Her immortality and made her thrall
To living death and pain perpetual;
  Which in her prescience she controllèd still,
  But her foresight could not forestall their will.

Ev'n in this thought through the dark night
      he stealeth,
A captive victor that hath lost in gain;
Bearing away the wound that nothing healeth,
The scar that will despite of cure remain;
Leaving his spoil perplexed in greater pain.
  She bears the load of lust he left behind,
  And he the burden of a guilty mind.

He like a thievish dog creeps sadly thence;
She like a wearied lamb lies panting there.
He scowls, and hates himself for his offense;
She desperate with her nails her flesh doth tear.
He faintly flies, sweating with guilty fear;
    She stays, exclaiming on the direful night;
    He runs, and chides his vanished loathed delight.

He thence departs a heavy convertite;
She there remains a hopeless castaway.
He in his speed looks for the morning light;
She prays she never may behold the day,
"For day," quoth she, "night's scapes doth open lay,
    And my true eyes have never practiced how
    To cloak offenses with a cunning brow.

"They think not but that every eye can see
The same disgrace which they themselves behold;
And therefore would they still in darkness be,
To have their unseen sin remain untold;
For they their guilt with weeping will unfold
    And grave, like water that doth eat in steel,
    Upon my cheeks what helpless shame I feel."

Here she exclaims against repose and rest,
And bids her eyes hereafter still be blind.
She wakes her heart by beating on her breast,
And bids it leap from thence, where it may find
Some purer chest to close so pure a mind.
 Frantic with grief thus breathes she forth her spite
 Against the unseen secrecy of night:

"O comfort-killing Night, image of hell,
Dim register and notary of shame,
Black stage for tragedies and murders fell,
Vast sin-concealing chaos, nurse of blame,
Blind muffled bawd, dark harbor for defame!
 Grim cave of death, whisp'ring conspirator
 With close-tongued treason and the ravisher!

"O hateful, vaporous, and foggy Night,
Since thou art guilty of my cureless crime,
Muster thy mists to meet the eastern light,
Make war against proportioned course of time;
Or if thou wilt permit the sun to climb
 His wonted height, yet ere he go to bed,
 Knit poisonous clouds about his golden head.

"With rotten damps ravish the morning air;
Let their exhaled unwholesome breaths make sick
The life of purity, the supreme fair,
Ere he arrive his weary noontide prick;
And let thy musty vapors march so thick
    That in their smoky ranks his smoth'red light
    May set at noon and make perpetual night.

"Were Tarquin Night, as he is but Night's child,
The silver-shining queen he would distain;
Her twinkling handmaids too, by him defiled,
Through Night's black bosom should not peep again.
So should I have co-partners in my pain;
    And fellowship in woe doth woe assuage,
    As palmers' chat makes short their pilgrimage;

*   *   *   *   *

"Why should the worm intrude the maiden bud?
Or hateful cuckoos hatch in sparrows' nests?
Or toads infect fair founts with venom mud?
Or tyrant folly lurk in gentle breasts?
Or kings be breakers of their own behests?
    But no perfection is so absolute
    That some impurity doth not pollute.

"The agèd man that coffers up his gold
Is plagued with cramps and gouts and painful fits,
And scarce hath eyes his treasure to behold,
But like still-pining Tantalus he sits
And useless barns the harvest of his wits,
    Having no other pleasure of his gain
    But torment that it cannot cure his pain.

"So then he hath it when he cannot use it,
And leaves it to be mast'red by his young,
Who in their pride do presently abuse it;
Their father was too weak, and they too strong,
To hold their cursèd-blessèd fortune long.
    The sweets we wish for turn to loathèd sours
    Even in the moment that we call them ours.

"Unruly blasts wait on the tender spring;
Unwholesome weeds take root with precious flow'rs;
The adder hisses where the sweet birds sing;
What virtue breeds iniquity devours.
We have no good that we can say is ours,
    But ill-annexèd opportunity
    Or kills his life or else his quality.

"O Opportunity, thy guilt is great!
'Tis thou that execut'st the traitor's treason;
Thou sets the wolf where he the lamb may get;
Whoever plots the sin, thou point'st the season.
'Tis thou that spurn'st at right, at law, at reason;
　　And in thy shady cell, where none may spy him,
　　Sits Sin, to seize the souls that wander by him.

"Thou mak'st the vestal violate her oath;
Thou blow'st the fire when temperance is thawed;
Thou smother'st honesty, thou murd'rest troth.
Thou foul abettor, thou notorious bawd,
Thou plantest scandal and displacest laud.
　　Thou ravisher, thou traitor, thou false thief,
　　Thy honey turns to gall, thy joy to grief.

"Thy secret pleasure turns to open shame,
Thy private feasting to a public fast,
Thy smoothing titles to a ragged name,
Thy sug'red tongue to bitter wormwood taste:
Thy violent vanities can never last.
　　How comes it then, vile Opportunity,
　　Being so bad, such numbers seek for thee?

"When wilt thou be the humble suppliant's friend
And bring him where his suit may be obtainèd?
When wilt thou sort an hour great strifes to end?
Or free that soul which wretchedness hath chainèd?
Give physic to the sick, ease to the painèd?
    The poor, lame, blind, halt, creep, cry out for thee;
    But they ne'er meet with Opportunity.

"The patient dies while the physician sleeps;
The orphan pines while the oppressor feeds;
Justice is feasting while the widow weeps;
Advice is sporting while infection breeds.
Thou grant'st no time for charitable deeds:
    Wrath, envy, treason, rape, and murder's rages,
    Thy heinous hours wait on them as their pages.

"When Truth and Virtue have to do with thee,
A thousand crosses keep them from thy aid.
They buy thy help; but Sin ne'er gives a fee,
He gratis comes; and thou art well apaid
As well to hear as grant what he hath said.
    My Collatine would else have come to me
    When Tarquin did, but he was stayed by thee.

"Guilty thou art of murder and of theft,
Guilty of perjury and subornation,
Guilty of treason, forgery, and shift,
Guilty of incest, that abomination:
An accessary by thine inclination
    To all sins past and all that are to come,
    From the creation to the general doom.

"Misshapen Time, copesmate of ugly Night,
Swift subtle post, carrier of grisly care,
Eater of youth, false slave to false delight,
Base watch of woes, sin's packhorse, virtue's snare!
Thou nursest all, and murd'rest all that are.
    O, hear me then, injurious shifting Time;
    Be guilty of my death, since of my crime.

"Why hath thy servant Opportunity
Betrayed the hours thou gav'st me to repose?
Canceled my fortunes, and enchainèd me
To endless date of never-ending woes?
Time's office is to fine the hate of foes,
    To eat up errors by opinion bred,
    Not spend the dowry of a lawful bed.

"Time's glory is to calm contending kings,
To unmask falsehood and bring truth to light,
To stamp the seal of time in agèd things,
To wake the morn and sentinel the night,
To wrong the wronger till he render right,
    To ruinate proud buildings with thy hours,
    And smear with dust their glitt'ring golden tow'rs;

"To fill with wormholes stately monuments,
To feed oblivion with decay of things,
To blot old books and alter their contents,
To pluck the quills from ancient ravens' wings,
To dry the old oak's sap and cherish springs,
    To spoil antiquities of hammered steel
    And turn the giddy round of Fortune's wheel;

"To show the beldame daughters of her daughter,
To make the child a man, the man a child,
To slay the tiger that doth live by slaughter,
To tame the unicorn and lion wild,
To mock the subtle in themselves beguiled,
    To cheer the ploughman with increaseful crops
    And waste huge stones with little water-drops.

"Why work'st thou mischief in thy pilgrimage,
Unless thou couldst return to make amends?
One poor retiring minute in an age
Would purchase thee a thousand thousand friends,
Lending him wit that to bad debtors lends.
    O this dread night, wouldst thou one hour come back,
    I could prevent this storm and shun thy wrack!"

* * * * *

But as the earth doth weep, the sun being set,
Each flower moist'ned like a melting eye,
Even so the maid with swelling drops 'gan wet
Her circled eyne, enforced by sympathy
Of those fair suns set in her mistress' sky,
    Who in a salt-waved ocean quench their light,
    Which makes the maid weep like the dewy night.

A pretty while these pretty creatures stand,
Like ivory conduits coral cisterns filling.
One justly weeps, the other takes in hand
No cause, but company, of her drops spilling.
Their gentle sex to weep are often willing,
    Grieving themselves to guess at others' smarts,
    And then they drown their eyes or break their
        hearts.

For men have marble, women waxen minds,
And therefore are they formed as marble will;
The weak oppressed, th' impression of strange kinds
Is formed in them by force, by fraud, or skill.
Then call them not the authors of their ill,
   No more than wax shall be accounted evil
   Wherein is stamped the semblance of a devil.

Their smoothness, like a goodly champain plain,
Lays open all the little worms that creep;
In men, as in a rough-grown grove, remain
Cave-keeping evils that obscurely sleep.
Through crystal walls each little mate will peep.
   Though men can cover crimes with bold stern looks,
   Poor women's faces are their own faults' books.

No man inveigh against the with'red flow'r,
But chide rough winter that the flow'r hath killed.
Nor that devoured, but that which doth devour,
Is worthy blame; O, let it not be hild
Poor women's faults that they are so fulfilled
   With men's abuses! those proud lords to blame
   Make weak-made women tenants to their shame.

The precedent whereof in Lucrece view,
Assailed by night with circumstances strong
Of present death, and shame that might ensue
By that her death, to do her husband wrong.
Such danger to resistance did belong
   That dying fear through all her body spread;
   And who cannot abuse a body dead?

By this, mild patience bid fair Lucrece speak
To the poor counterfeit of her complaining.
"My girl," quoth she, "on what occasion break
Those tears from thee that down thy cheeks are raining?
If thou dost weep for grief of my sustaining,
   Know, gentle wench, it small avails my mood;
   If tears could help, mine own would do me good.

"But tell me, girl, when went" (and there she stayed
Till after a deep groan) "Tarquin from hence?"
"Madam, ere I was up," replied the maid,
"The more to blame my sluggard negligence.
Yet with the fault I thus far can dispense:
   Myself was stirring ere the break of day,
   And ere I rose was Tarquin gone away.

"But, lady, if your maid may be so bold,
She would request to know your heaviness."
"O, peace," quoth Lucrece. "If it should be told,
The repetition cannot make it less;
For more it is than I can well express,
   And that deep torture may be called a hell
   When more is felt than one hath power to tell.

"Go get me hither paper, ink, and pen;
Yet save that labor, for I have them here.
What should I say? One of my husband's men
Bid thou be ready by and by to bear
A letter to my lord, my love, my dear.
   Bid him with speed prepare to carry it;
   The cause craves haste, and it will soon be writ."

Her maid is gone, and she prepares to write,
First hovering o'er the paper with her quill.
Conceit and grief an eager combat fight;
What wit sets down is blotted straight with will.
This is too curious good, this blunt and ill.
   Much like a press of people at a door,
   Throng her inventions, which shall go before.

At last she thus begins: "Thou worthy lord
Of that unworthy wife that greeteth thee,
Health to thy person! next vouchsafe t' afford
(If ever, love, thy Lucrece thou wilt see)
Some present speed to come and visit me.
  So I commend me, from our house in grief.
  My woes are tedious, though my words are brief."

Here folds she up the tenure of her woe,
Her certain sorrow writ uncertainly.
By this short schedule Collatine may know
Her grief, but not her grief's true quality;
She dares not thereof make discovery,
  Lest he should hold it her own gross abuse
  Ere she with blood had stained her stained excuse.

Besides, the life and feeling of her passion
She hoards, to spend when he is by to hear her,
When sighs and groans and tears may grace the
      fashion
Of her disgrace, the better so to clear her
From that suspicion which the world might bear her.
  To shun this blot, she would not blot the letter
  With words till action might become them better.

To see sad sights moves more than hear them told,
For then the eye interprets to the ear
The heavy motion that it doth behold
When every part a part of woe doth bear.
'Tis but a part of sorrow that we hear.
  Deep sounds make lesser noise than shallow fords,
  And sorrow ebbs, being blown with winds of words.

*   *   *   *   *

At last she calls to mind where hangs a piece
Of skillful painting, made for Priam's Troy,
Before the which is drawn the power of Greece,
For Helen's rape the city to destroy,
Threat'ning cloud-kissing Ilion with annoy;
  Which the conceited painter drew so proud
  As heaven, it seemed, to kiss the turrets bowed.

*   *   *   *   *

To this well-painted piece is Lucrece come,
To find a face where all distress is stelled.
Many she sees where cares have carvèd some,
But none where all distress and dolor dwelled
Till she despairing Hecuba beheld,
  Staring on Priam's wounds with her old eyes,
  Which bleeding under Pyrrhus' proud foot lies.

In her the painter had anatomized
Time's ruin, beauty's wrack, and grim care's reign;
Her cheeks with chops and wrinkles were disguised;
Of what she was no semblance did remain.
Her blue blood, changed to black in every vein,
    Wanting the spring that those shrunk pipes had fed,
    Showed life imprisoned in a body dead.

On this sad shadow Lucrece spends her eyes
And shapes her sorrow to the beldame's woes,
Who nothing wants to answer but her cries
And bitter words to ban her cruel foes.
The painter was no god to lend her those;
    And therefore Lucrece swears he did her wrong
    To give her so much grief and not a tongue.

"Poor instrument," quoth she, "without a sound:
I'll tune thy woes with my lamenting tongue,
And drop sweet balm in Priam's painted wound,
And rail on Pyrrhus that hath done him wrong,
And with my tears quench Troy that burns so long,
    And with my knife scratch out the angry eyes
    Of all the Greeks that are thine enemies."

*　*　*　*　*

Thus ebbs and flows the current of her sorrow,
And time doth weary time with her complaining.
She looks for night, and then she longs for morrow,
And both she thinks too long with her remaining.
Short time seems long in sorrow's sharp sustaining;
    Though woe be heavy, yet it seldom sleeps,
    And they that watch see time how slow it creeps;

Which all this time hath overslipped her thought
That she with painted images hath spent,
Being from the feeling of her own grief brought
By deep surmise of others' detriment,
Losing her woes in shows of discontent.
    It easeth some, though none it ever curèd.
    To think their dolor others have endurèd.

*   *   *   *   *

SONGS AND
SPEECHES

WHO IS SILVIA?

Who is Silvia, what is she,
    That all our swains commend her?
Holy, fair, and wise is she;
    The heaven such grace did lend her,
That she might admirèd be.

Is she kind as she is fair?
    For beauty lives with kindness.
Love doth to her eyes repair,
    To help him of his blindness,
And, being helped, inhabits there.

Then to Silvia let us sing,
    That Silvia is excelling;
She excels each mortal thing
    Upon the dull earth dwelling.
To her let us garlands bring.

Two Gentlemen of Verona, IV.ii.

SIGH NO MORE, LADIES

Sigh no more, ladies, sigh no more,
   Men were deceivers ever,
One foot in sea, and one on shore,
   To one thing constant never.
     Then sigh not so,
     But let them go,
   And be you blithe and bonny,
Converting all your sounds of woe
   Into hey nonny, nonny.

Sing no more ditties, sing no moe,
   Of dumps so dull and heavy;
The fraud of men was ever so,
   Since summer first was leavy.
     Then sigh not so,
     But let them go,
   And be you blithe and bonny,
Converting all your sounds of woe
   Into hey nonny, nonny.

190   *Much Ado About Nothing*, II.iii.

IT WAS A LOVER AND HIS LASS

It was a lover and his lass,
　　With a hey, and a ho, and a hey nonino,
That o'er the green cornfield did pass
　　In springtime, the only pretty ringtime,
When birds do sing, hey ding a ding, ding.
Sweet lovers love the spring.

Between the acres of the rye,
　　With a hey, and a ho, and a hey nonino,
These pretty country folks would lie
　　In springtime, &c.

This carol they began that hour,
　　With a hey, and a ho, and a hey nonino,
How that a life was but a flower
　　In springtime, &c.

And therefore take the present time,
　　With a hey, and a ho, and a hey nonino,
For love is crownèd with the prime
　　In springtime, &c.

As You Like It, V.iii.　　　　　　　　191

LAWN AS WHITE AS DRIVEN SNOW

Lawn as white as driven snow,
Cypress black as e'er was crow,
Gloves as sweet as damask roses,
Masks for faces, and for noses;
Bugle-bracelet, necklace-amber,
Perfume for a lady's chamber;
Golden quoifs and stomachers
For my lads to give their dears;
Pins and poking sticks of steel;
What maids lack from head to heel!
Come buy of me, come, come buy, come buy,
Buy lads, or else your lasses cry; come buy!

HARK, HARK, THE LARK

Hark, hark, the lark at heaven's gate sings,
   And Phoebus gins arise,
His steeds to water at those springs
   On chaliced flowers that lies;
And winking Mary-buds begin
   To ope their golden eyes.
With every thing that pretty is,
   My lady sweet, arise,
     Arise, arise!

Cymbeline, II.iii.

OBERON I know a bank where the wild thyme blows,
   Where oxlips and the nodding violet grows,
   Quite overcanopied with luscious woodbine,
   With sweet musk roses, and with eglantine.
   There sleeps Titania sometime of the night,
   Lulled in these flowers with dances and delight;
   And there the snake throws her enameled skin,
   Weed wide enough to wrap a fairy in.
   And with the juice of this I'll streak her eyes,
   And make her full of hateful fantasies.
   Take thou some of it, and seek through this grove.
   A sweet Athenian lady is in love
   With a disdainful youth. Anoint his eyes;
   But do it when the next thing he espies
   May be the lady. Thou shalt know the man
   By the Athenian garments he hath on.
   Effect it with some care that he may prove
   More fond on her than she upon her love:
   And look thou meet me ere the first cock crow.

TELL ME WHERE IS FANCY BRED

Tell me where is fancy bred,
Or in the heart, or in the head?
How begot, how nourishèd?
   Reply, reply.
It is engend'red in the eyes,
With gazing fed, and fancy dies
In the cradle where it lies.
   Let us all ring fancy's knell.
   I'll begin it – Ding, dong, bell.
   Ding, dong, bell.

The Merchant of Venice, III.ii.

ENOBARBUS The barge she sat in, like a burnished
        throne,
    Burned on the water: the poop was beaten gold;
    Purple the sails, and so perfumèd that
    The winds were lovesick with them; the oars were
        silver,
    Which to the tune of flutes kept stroke and made
    The water which they beat to follow faster,
    As amorous of their strokes. For her own person,
    It beggared all description: she did lie
    In her pavilion, cloth-of-gold of tissue,
    O'erpicturing that Venus where we see
    The fancy outwork nature: on each side her
    Stood pretty dimpled boys, like smiling Cupids,
    With divers-colored fans, whose wind did seem
    To glow the delicate cheeks which they did cool,
    And what they undid did.

AGRIPPA   O, rare for Antony.

ENOBARBUS Her gentlewomen, like the Nereides,
   So many mermaids, tended her i' th' eyes,
   And made their bends adornings. At the helm
   A seeming mermaid steers: the silken tackle
   Swell with the touches of those flower-soft hands,
   That yarely frame the office. From the barge
   A strange invisible perfume hits the sense
   Of the adjacent wharfs. The city cast
   Her people out upon her; and Antony,
   Enthroned i' th' marketplace, did sit alone,
   Whistling to th' air; which, but for vacancy,
   Had gone to gaze on Cleopatra too,
   And made a gap in nature.

Antony and Cleopatra, II.ii.

PARDON, GODDESS OF THE NIGHT

Pardon, goddess of the night,
Those that slew thy virgin knight;
For the which, with songs of woe,
Round about her tomb they go.
Midnight, assist our moan;
Help us to sigh and groan,
  Heavily, heavily.
Graves, yawn and yield your dead,
Till death be utterèd,
  Heavily, heavily.

WHEN DAFFODILS BEGIN TO PEER

When daffodils begin to peer,
    With heigh the doxy over the dale,
Why, then comes in the sweet o' the year,
    For the red blood reigns in the winter's pale.

The white sheet bleaching on the hedge,
    With heigh the sweet birds, O how they sing!
Doth set my pugging tooth an edge,
    For a quart of ale is a dish for a king.

The lark, that tirra-lirra chants,
    With heigh, with heigh, the thrust and the jay!
Are summer songs for me and my aunts
    While we lie tumbling in the hay.

But shall I go mourn for that, my dear?
    The pale moon shines by night;
And when I wander here and there
    I then do most go right.
If tinkers may have leave to live,
    And bear the sow-skin budget,
Then my account I well may give,
    And in the stocks avouch it.

The Winter's Tale, IV.ii.   199

ORSINO If music be the food of love, play on,
    Give me excess of it, that, surfeiting,
    The appetite may sicken, and so die.
    That strain again! It had a dying fall;
    O, it came o'er my ear like the sweet sound
    That breathes upon a bank of violets,
    Stealing and giving odor. Enough, no more!
    'Tis not so sweet now as it was before.
    O spirit of love, how quick and fresh art thou,
    That, notwithstanding thy capacity,
    Receiveth as the sea. Nought enters there,
    Of what validity and pitch soe'er,
    But falls into abatement and low price
    Even in a minute. So full of shapes is fancy
    That it alone is high fantastical.

LORENZO The moon shines bright. In such a night as
    this,
  When the sweet wind did gently kiss the trees
  And they did make no noise, in such a night
  Troilus methinks mounted the Troyan walls,
  And sighed his soul toward the Grecian tents
  Where Cressid lay that night.

JESSICA   In such a night
  Did Thisbe fearfully o'ertrip the dew,
  And saw the lion's shadow ere himself,
  And ran dismayed away.

LORENZO   In such a night
  Stood Dido with a willow in her hand
  Upon the wild sea banks, and waft her love
  To come again to Carthage.

LORENZO How sweet the moonlight sleeps upon this
    bank!
  Here will we sit and let the sounds of music
  Creep in our ears; soft stillness and the night
  Become the touches of sweet harmony.
  Sit, Jessica. Look how the floor of heaven
  Is thick inlaid with patens of bright gold.
  There's not the smallest orb which thou behold'st
  But in his motion like an angel sings,
  Still quiring to the young-eyed cherubins;
  Such harmony is in immortal souls,
  But whilst this muddy vesture of decay
  Doth grossly close it in, we cannot hear it.

VIOLA Make me a willow cabin at your gate
And call upon my soul within the house;
Write loyal cantons of contemnèd love
And sing them loud even in the dead of night;
Hallo your name to the reverberate hills
And make the babbling gossip of the air
Cry out "Olivia!" O, you should not rest
Between the elements of air and earth
But you should pity me.

HONOR, RICHES, MARRIAGE BLESSING

Honor, riches, marriage blessing,
Long continuance, and increasing,
Hourly joys be still upon you!
Juno sings her blessings on you.
Earth's increase, foison plenty,
Barns and garners never empty,
Vines with clust'ring bunches growing,
Plants with goodly burden bowing;
Spring come to you at the farthest
In the very end of harvest.
Scarcity and want shall shun you,
Ceres' blessing so is on you.

O MISTRESS MINE, WHERE ARE YOU ROAMING?

O mistress mine, where are you roaming?
O, stay and hear, your true-love's coming,
   That can sing both high and low.
Trip no further, pretty sweeting;
Journeys end in lovers meeting,
   Every wise man's son doth know.

What is love? 'Tis not hereafter;
Present mirth hath present laughter;
   What's to come is still unsure:
In delay there lies no plenty;
Then come kiss me, sweet, and twenty,
   Youth's a stuff will not endure.

Twelfth Night, II.iii.

ROMEO He jests at scars that never felt a wound.
                [Enter Juliet at a window.]
But soft! What light through yonder window breaks?
It is the East, and Juliet is the sun!
Arise, fair sun, and kill the envious moon,
Who is already sick and pale with grief
That thou her maid art far more fair than she.
Be not her maid, since she is envious.
Her vestal livery is but sick and green,
And none but fools do wear it. Cast it off.
It is my lady! O, it is my love!
O, that she knew she were!
She speaks, yet she says nothing. What of that?
Her eye discourses; I will answer it.
I am too bold; 'tis not to me she speaks.
Two of the fairest stars in all the heaven,
Having some business, do entreat her eyes
To twinkle in their spheres till they return.
What if her eyes were there, they in her head?
The brightness of her cheek would shame those stars
As daylight doth a lamp; her eyes in heaven
Would through the airy region stream so bright
That birds would sing and think it were not night.
See how she leans her cheek upon her hand!
O, that I were a glove upon that hand,
That I might touch that cheek!
JULIET   Ay me!

ROMEO   She speaks.

O, speak again, bright angel, for thou art
As glorious to this night, being o'er my head,
As is a wingèd messenger of heaven
Unto the white-upturnèd wond'ring eyes
Of mortals that fall back to gaze on him
When he bestrides the lazy puffing clouds
And sails upon the bosom of the air.

JULIET O Romeo, Romeo! Wherefore art thou Romeo?
Deny thy father and refuse thy name;
Or, if thou wilt not, be but sworn my love,
And I'll no longer be a Capulet.

ROMEO [*Aside*] Shall I hear more, or shall I speak
   at this?

JULIET 'Tis but thy name that is my enemy.
Thou art thyself, though not a Montague.
What's Montague? It is nor hand, nor foot,
Nor arm, nor face. O, be some other name
Belonging to a man.
What's in a name? That which we call a rose
By any other word would smell as sweet.
So Romeo would, were he not Romeo called,
Retain that dear perfection which he owes
Without that title. Romeo, doff thy name;
And for thy name, which is no part of thee,
Take all myself.

Romeo and Juliet, II.ii.   207

COME UNTO THESE YELLOW SANDS
Ariel's Song

Come unto these yellow sands,
   And then take hands.
Curtsied when you have and kissed
   The wild waves whist,
Foot it featly here and there;
And, sweet sprites, the burden bear.
   Hark, hark!
     Burden, dispersedly. Bow, wow!
   The watchdogs bark.
     [*Burden, dispersedly.*] Bow, wow!
   Hark, hark! I hear
   The strain of strutting chanticleer
     Cry cock-a-diddle-dow.

FULL FATHOM FIVE THY FATHER LIES
Ariel's Song

Full fathom five thy father lies;
   Of his bones are coral made;
Those are pearls that were his eyes;
   Nothing of him that doth fade
But doth suffer a sea change
Into something rich and strange.
Sea nymphs hourly ring his knell:
        Burden. Ding-dong.
Hark! Now I hear them – ding-dong bell.

The Tempest, I.ii.

THE MASTER, THE SWABBER, THE BOATSWAIN, AND I

The master, the swabber, the boatswain, and I,
    The gunner, and his mate,
Loved Mall, Meg, and Marian, and Margery,
   But none of us cared for Kate.
   For she had a tongue with a tang,
   Would cry to a sailor "Go hang!"
She loved not the savor of tar nor of pitch;
Yet a tailor might scratch her where'er she did itch.
   Then to sea, boys, and let her go hang!

FAIRY SONG

1ST FAIRY	You spotted snakes with double tongue,
	    Thorny hedgehogs, be not seen;
	Newts and blindworms, do no wrong,
	    Come not near our Fairy Queen.

CHORUS	Philomele, with melody
	    Sing in our sweet lullaby;
	Lulla, lulla, lullaby, lulla, lulla, lullaby:
	      Never harm
	      Nor spell nor charm,
	    Come our lovely lady nigh;
	    So, good night, with lullaby.

1ST FAIRY	Weaving spiders, come not here;
	    Hence, you long-legged spinners, hence!
	Beetles black, approach not near;
	    Worm nor snail, do no offense.

CHORUS	Philomele, with melody, &c.
2ND FAIRY	Hence, away! Now all is well. One aloof stand sentinel.

WHERE THE BEE SUCKS
Ariel's Song

Where the bee sucks, there suck I;
In a cowslip's bell I lie;
There I couch when owls do cry.
On the bat's back I do fly
After summer merrily.
Merrily, merrily shall I live now
Under the blossom that hangs on the bough.

OVER HILL, OVER DALE

PUCK   How now, spirit! Whither wander you?

FAIRY   Over hill, over dale,
                  Thorough bush, thorough brier,
              Over park, over pale,
                  Thorough flood, thorough fire,
              I do wander everywhere,
              Swifter than the moon's sphere;
              And I serve the Fairy Queen,
              To dew her orbs upon the green.
              The cowslips tall her pensioners be:
              In their gold coats spots you see;
              Those be rubies, fairy favors,
              In those freckles live their savors.
         I must go seek some dewdrops here,
         And hang a pearl in every cowslip's ear.
         Farewell, thou lob of spirits; I'll be gone.
         Our Queen and all her elves come here anon.

A Midsummer Night's Dream, II.i.   213

UNDER THE GREENWOOD TREE

Under the greenwood tree
   Who loves to lie with me,
And turn his merry note
   Unto the sweet bird's throat,
Come hither, come hither, come hither.
   Here shall he see no enemy
But winter and rough weather.

Who doth ambition shun
   And loves to live i' th' sun,
Seeking the food he eats,
   And pleased with what he gets,
Come hither, come hither, come hither.
   Here shall he see no enemy
But winter and rough weather.

WHEN THAT I WAS AND A
LITTLE TINY BOY

When that I was and a little tiny boy,
  With hey, ho, the wind and the rain,
A foolish thing was but a toy,
  For the rain it raineth every day.

But when I came to man's estate,
  With hey, ho, the wind and the rain,
'Gainst knaves and thieves men shut their gate,
  For the rain it raineth every day.

But when I came, alas, to wive,
  With hey, ho, the wind and the rain,
By swaggering could I never thrive,
  For the rain it raineth every day.

But when I came unto my beds,
  With hey, ho, the wind and the rain,
With tosspots still had drunken heads,
  For the rain it raineth every day.

A great while ago the world begun,
  Hey, ho, the wind and the rain;
But that's all one, our play is done,
  And we'll strive to please you every day.

Twelfth Night, V.i.

TAKE, O, TAKE THOSE LIPS AWAY

Take, O, take those lips away,
That so sweetly were forsworn;
And those eyes, the break of day,
Lights that do mislead the morn;
But my kisses bring again, bring again;
Seals of love, but sealed in vain, sealed in vain.

WHEN DAISIES PIED AND VIOLETS BLUE

[*Spring.*] When daisies pied and violets blue
      And lady-smocks all silver-white
And cuckoo-buds of yellow hue
      Do paint the meadows with delight,
The cuckoo then, on every tree,
Mocks married men; for thus sings he,
      "Cuckoo!
Cuckoo, cuckoo!" O word of fear,
Unpleasing to a married ear!

When shepherds pipe on oaten straws,
      And merry larks are ploughmen's clocks,
When turtles tread, and rooks, and daws,
      And maidens bleach their summer
         smocks,
The cuckoo then, on every tree,
Mocks married men; for thus sings he,
      "Cuckoo!
Cuckoo, cuckoo!" O word of fear,
Unpleasing to a married ear!

[*Winter.*] When icicles hang by the wall,
    And Dick the shepherd blows his nail,
And Tom bears logs into the hall,
    And milk comes frozen home in pail,
When blood is nipped, and ways be foul,
Then nightly sings the staring owl,
        "Tu-whit,
Tu-who!" a merry note,
While greasy Joan doth keel the pot.

When all aloud the wind doth blow,
    And coughing drowns the parson's saw,
And birds sit brooding in the snow,
    And Marian's nose looks red and raw,
When roasted crabs hiss in the bowl,
Then nightly sings the staring owl,
        "Tu-whit,
Tu-who!" a merry note,
While greasy Joan doth keel the pot.

PERDITA   Out, alas!
You'd be so lean that blasts of January
Would blow you through and through. [*To
      Florizel*]
    Now, my fair'st friend,
I would I had some flow'rs o' th' spring, that might
Become your time of day – [*to Shepherdesses*] and
      yours, and yours,
That wear upon your virgin branches yet
Your maidenheads growing. O Proserpina,
For the flow'rs now, that, frighted, thou let'st fall
From Dis's wagon! Daffodils,
That come before the swallow dares, and take
The winds of March with beauty; violets, dim,
But sweeter than the lids of Juno's eyes,
Or Cytherea's breath; pale primroses,
That die unmarried ere they can behold
Bright Phoebus in his strength (a malady
Most incident to maids); bold oxlips, and
The crown imperial; lilies of all kinds,
The flower-de-luce being one. O, these I lack
To make you garlands of, and my sweet friend,
To strew him o'er and o'er!

FLORIZEL   What, like a corse?

PERDITA No, like a bank for Love to lie and play on;
  Not like a corse; or if, not to be buried,
  But quick and in mine arms. Come, take you flow'rs;
  Methinks I play as I have seen them do
  In Whitsun pastorals; sure this robe of mine
  Does change my disposition.

FLORIZEL   What you do
  Still betters what is done. When you speak, sweet,
  I'd have you do it ever; when you sing,
  I'd have you buy and sell so; so give alms,
  Pray so; and for the ord'ring your affairs,
  To sing them too. When you do dance, I wish you
  A wave o' th' sea, that you might ever do
  Nothing but that – move still, still so,
  And own no other function. Each your doing,
  So singular in each particular,
  Crowns what you are doing in the present deeds,
  That all your acts are queens.

LEAR O! reason not the need; our basest beggars
      Are in the poorest thing superfluous:
      Allow not nature more than nature needs,
      Man's life is cheap as beast's. Thou art a lady:
      If only to go warm were gorgeous,
      Why, nature needs not what thou gorgeous wear'st,
      Which scarcely keeps thee warm. But, for true
          need, –
      You Heavens, give me that patience, patience I
          need! –
      You see me here, you Gods, a poor old man,
      As full of grief as age; wretched in both!
      If it be you that stirs these daughters' hearts
      Against their father, fool me not so much
      To bear it tamely; touch me with noble anger,
      And let not women's weapons, water-drops,
      Stain my man's cheeks! No, you unnatural hags,
      I will have such revenges on you both
      That all the world shall – I will do such things,
      What they are, yet I know not, but they shall be
      The terrors of the earth. You think I'll weep;
      No, I'll not weep:
      I have full cause of weeping, [*Storm heard at a
          distance.*] but this heart
      Shall break into a hundred thousand flaws
      Or ere I'll weep. O Fool! I shall go mad.

King Lear, II.iv.   221

LEAR Thou think'st 'tis much that this contentious
        storm
      Invades us to the skin: so 'tis to thee;
      But where the greater malady is fix'd,
      The lesser is scarce felt. Thou'ldst shun a bear;
      But if thy flight lay toward the roaring sea,
      Thou'ldst meet the bear i' th' mouth. When the
        mind's free
      The body's delicate; this tempest in my mind
      Doth from my senses take all feeling else
      Save what beats there – filial ingratitude!
      Is it not as this mouth should tear this hand
      For lifting food to 't? But I will punish home:
      No, I will weep no more. In such a night
      To shut me out? Pour on; I will endure.
      In such a night as this? O Regan, Goneril!
      Your old kind father, whose frank heart gave all –
      O! that way madness lies; let me shun that;
      No more of that.

KENT   Good my Lord, enter here.

LEAR Prithee, go in thyself; seek thine own ease:
    This tempest will not give me leave to ponder
    On things would hurt me more. But I'll go in.
    [*To the Fool.*] In, boy; go first. You houseless
        poverty, –
    Nay, get thee in. I'll pray, and then I'll sleep.
                                    [*Fool goes in.*
    Poor naked wretches, wheresoe'er you are,
    That bide the pelting of this pitiless storm,
    How shall your houseless heads and unfed sides,
    Your loop'd and window'd raggedness, defend you
    From seasons such as these? O! I have ta'en
    Too little care of this. Take physic, Pomp;
    Expose thyself to feel what wretches feel,
    That thou mayst shake the superflux to them,
    And show the Heavens more just.

EDGAR [*Within.*] Fathom and half, fathom and half!
    Poor Tom!   *The Fool runs out from the hovel.*

FOOL Come not in here, Nuncle; here's a spirit.
    Help me! help me!

RICHARD What must the King do now? Must he
    submit?
  The King shall do it. Must he be deposed?
  The King shall be contented. Must he lose
  The name of king? a God's name, let it go.
  I'll give my jewels for a set of beads;
  My gorgeous palace for a hermitage;
  My gay apparel for an almsman's gown;
  My figured goblets for a dish of wood;
  My scepter for a palmer's walking-staff;
  My subjects for a pair of carvèd saints;
  And my large kingdom for a little grave,
  A little, little grave, an obscure grave;
  Or I'll be buried in the King's highway,
  Some way of common trade, where subjects' feet
  May hourly trample on their sovereign's head;
  For on my heart they tread now whilst I live,
  And buried once, why not upon my head?
  Aumerle, thou weep'st, my tender-hearted cousin:
  We'll make foul weather with despisèd tears;
  Our sighs and they shall lodge the summer corn,
  And make a dearth in this revolting land:
  Or shall we play the wantons with our woes
  And make some pretty match with shedding tears,
  As thus, to drop them still upon one place,
  Till they have fretted us a pair of graves
  Within the earth; and, therein laid, "there lies

Two kinsmen digged their graves with weeping eyes":
Would not this ill do well? Well, well, I see
I talk but idly, and you laugh at me.
Most mighty prince, my Lord Northumberland,
What says King Bolingbroke? Will his Majesty
Give Richard leave to live till Richard die?
You make a leg, and Bolingbroke says "Ay."

Richard II, III.iii.   225

JACQUES   All the world's a stage,
  And all the men and women merely players;
  They have their exits and their entrances,
  And one man in his time plays many parts,
  His acts being seven ages. At first, the infant,
  Mewling and puking in the nurse's arms.
  Then the whining schoolboy, with his satchel
  And shining morning face, creeping like snail
  Unwillingly to school. And then the lover,
  Sighing like furnace, with a woeful ballad
  Made to his mistress' eyebrow. Then a soldier,
  Full of strange oaths and bearded like the pard,
  Jealous in honor, sudden and quick in quarrel,
  Seeking the bubble reputation
  Even in the cannon's mouth. And then the justice,
  In fair round belly with good capon lined,
  With eyes severe and beard of formal cut,
  Full of wise saws and modern instances;
  And so he plays his part. The sixth age shifts
  Into the lean and slippered pantaloon,
  With spectacles on nose and pouch on side;
  His youthful hose, well saved, a world too wide
  For his shrunk shank, and his big manly voice,
  Turning again toward childish treble, pipes
  And whistles in his sound. Last scene of all,
  That ends this strange eventful history,
  Is second childishness and mere oblivion,
  Sans teeth, sans eyes, sans taste, sans everything.

226   *As You Like It*, II.vii.

PORTIA The quality of mercy is not strained;
It droppeth as the gentle rain from heaven
Upon the place beneath. It is twice blest;
It blesseth him that gives and him that takes.
'Tis mightiest in the mightiest; it becomes
The thronèd monarch better than his crown.
His scepter shows the force of temporal power,
The attribute to awe and majesty,
Wherein doth sit the dread and fear of kings;
But mercy is above this scept'red sway;
It is enthronèd in the hearts of kings,
It is an attribute to God himself,
And earthly power doth then show likest God's
When mercy seasons justice. Therefore, Jew,
Though justice be thy plea, consider this:
That, in the course of justice, none of us
Should see salvation. We do pray for mercy,
And that same prayer doth teach us all to render
The deeds of mercy. I have spoke thus much
To mitigate the justice of thy plea;
Which if thou follow, this strict court of Venice
Must needs give sentence 'gainst the merchant
    there.

The Merchant of Venice, IV.i.   227

Now all the youth of England are on fire,
And silken dálliance in the wardrobe lies;
Now thrive the armorers, and honor's thought
Reigns solely in the breast of every man.
They sell the pasture now, to buy the horse;
Following the mirror of all Christian kings
With wingèd heels, as English Mercuries.
For now sits Expectation in the air
And hides a sword, from hilts unto the point,
With crowns imperial, crowns and coronets
Promised to Harry and his followers.
The French, advised by good intelligence
Of this most dreadful preparation,
Shake in their fear, and with pale policy
Seek to divert the English purposes.
O England, model to thy inward greatness,
Like little body with a mighty heart,
What mightst thou do, that honor would thee do,
Were all thy children kind and natural!
But see, thy fault France hath in thee found out —
A nest of hollow bosoms — which he fills
With treacherous crowns; and three corrupted men —
One, Richard Earl of Cambridge, and the second,
Henry Lord Scroop of Masham, and the third,
Sir Thomas Grey, knight, of Northumberland —
Have, for the gilt of France (O guilt indeed!),
Confirmed conspiracy with fearful France,

And by their hands this grace of kings must die,
If hell and treason hold their promises,
Ere he take ship for France, and in Southampton.
Linger your patience on, and we'll digest
Th' abuse of distance; force a play: —
The sum is paid; the traitors are agreed;
The King is set from London; and the scene
Is now transported, gentles, to Southampton.
There is the playhouse now, there must you sit,
And thence to France shall we convey you safe
And bring you back, charming the narrow seas
To give you gentle pass; for, if we may,
We'll not offend one stomach with our play.
But, till the King come forth, and not till then,
Unto Southampton do we shift our scene.

Henry V, II, Chorus

KING It earns me not if men my garments wear;
   Such outward things dwell not in my desires:
   But if it be a sin to covet honor,
   I am the most offending soul alive.
   No, faith, my coz, wish not a man from England.
   God's peace! I would not lose so great an honor
   As one man more methinks would share from me
   For the best hope I have. O, do not wish one more!
   Rather proclaim it, Westmoreland, through my host,
   That he which hath no stomach to this fight,
   Let him depart; his passport shall be made,
   And crowns for convoy put into his purse;
   We would not die in that man's company
   That fears his fellowship to die with us.
   This day is called the Feast of Crispian:
   He that outlives this day, and comes safe home,
   Will stand a-tiptoe when this day is named,
   And rouse him at the name of Crispian.
   He that shall see this day, and live old age,
   Will yearly on the vigil feast his neighbors
   And say, "Tomorrow is Saint Crispian."
   Then will he strip his sleeve and show his scars,
   And say, "These wounds I had on Crispin's day."
   Old men forget; yet all shall be forgot,
   But he'll remember, with advantages,
   What feats he did that day. Then shall our names,
   Familiar in his mouth as household words —

Harry the King, Bedford and Exeter,
Warwick and Talbot, Salisbury and Gloucester –
Be in their flowing cups freshly rememb'red.
This story shall the good man teach his son;
And Crispin Crispian shall ne'er go by,
From this day to the ending of the world,
But we in it shall be rememberèd –
We few, we happy few, we band of brothers;
For he today that sheds his blood with me
Shall be my brother; be he ne'er so vile,
This day shall gentle his condition.
And gentlemen in England, now abed,
Shall think themselves accursed they were not here;
And hold their manhoods cheap whiles any speaks
That fought with us upon Saint Crispin's day.

Henry V, IV.iii.

KING Once more unto the breach, dear friends, once
        more;
    Or close the wall up with our English dead!
    In peace there's nothing so becomes a man
    As modest stillness and humility;
    But when the blast of war blows in our ears,
    Then imitate the action of the tiger:
    Stiffen the sinews, conjure up the blood,
    Disguise fair nature with hard-favored rage;
    Then lend the eye a terrible aspect:
    Let it pry through the portage of the head
    Like the brass cannon; let the brow o'erwhelm it
    As fearfully as doth a gallèd rock
    O'erhang and jutty his confounded base,
    Swilled with the wild and wasteful ocean.
    Now set the teeth, and stretch the nostril wide,
    Hold hard the breath, and bend up every spirit
    To his full height! On, on, you noble English,
    Whose blood is fet from fathers of war-proof!
    Fathers that like so many Alexanders
    Have in these parts from morn till even fought
    And sheathed their swords for lack of argument.
    Dishonor not your mothers; now attest
    That those whom you called fathers did beget you!
    Be copy now to men of grosser blood
    And teach them how to war! And you, good yeomen,
    Whose limbs were made in England, show us here

The mettle of your pasture. Let us swear
That you are worth your breeding; which I doubt not,
For there is none of you so mean and base
That hath not noble luster in your eyes.
I see you stand like greyhounds in the slips,
Straining upon the start. The game's afoot!
Follow your spirit; and upon this charge,
Cry, "God for Harry, England and Saint George!"

Henry V, III.i.

GAUNT Methinks I am a prophet new inspired,
    And thus éxpiring do foretell of him:
    His rash fierce blaze of riot cannot last,
    For violent fires soon burn out themselves.
    Small showers last long, but sudden storms are
        short;
    He tires betimes that spurs too fast betimes;
    With eager feeding, food doth choke the feeder.
    Light vanity, insatiate cormorant,
    Consuming means, soon preys upon itself.
    This royal throne of kings, this scept'red isle,
    This earth of majesty, this seat of Mars,
    This other Eden, demi-paradise,
    This fortress built by Nature for herself
    Against infection and the hand of war,
    This happy breed of men, this little world,
    This precious stone set in the silver sea
    Which serves it in the office of a wall,
    Or as a moat defensive to a house,
    Against the envy of less happier lands,
    This blessed plot, this earth, this realm, this
        England,
    This nurse, this teeming womb of royal kings,
    Feared by their breed, and famous by their birth,
    Renownèd for their deeds as far from home,
    For Christian service and true chivalry,
    As is the sepulcher in stubborn Jewry

Of the world's ransom, blessed Mary's son,
This land of such dear souls, this dear dear land –
Dear for her reputation through the world –
Is now leased out – I die pronouncing it –
Like to a tenement or pelting farm.
England, bound in with the triumphant sea,
Whose rocky shore beats back the envious siege
Of wat'ry Neptune, is now bound in with shame,
With inky blots, and rotten parchment bonds.
That England that was wont to conquer others
Hath made a shameful conquest of itself.
Ah! would the scandal vanish with my life,
How happy then were my ensuing death!

COME AWAY, COME AWAY, DEATH

Come away, come away, death,
 And in sad cypress let me be laid.
Fly away, fly away, breath;
 I am slain by a fair cruel maid.
My shroud of white, stuck all with yew,
  O, prepare it.
My part of death, no one so true
  Did share it.

Not a flower, not a flower sweet,
 On my black coffin let there be strown;
Not a friend, not a friend greet
 My poor corpse, where my bones shall be
  thrown.
A thousand thousand sighs to save,
  Lay me, O, where
Sad true lover never find my grave,
  To weep there.

HAMLET To be, or not to be: that is the question:
Whether 'tis nobler in the mind to suffer
The slings and arrows of outrageous fortune,
Or to take arms against a sea of troubles,
And by opposing end them. To die, to sleep –
No more – and by a sleep to say we end
The heartache, and the thousand natural shocks
That flesh is heir to! 'Tis a consummation
Devoutly to be wished. To die, to sleep –
To sleep – perchance to dream: ay, there's the rub,
For in that sleep of death what dreams may come
When we have shuffled off this mortal coil,
Must give us pause. There's the respect
That makes calamity of so long life:
For who would bear the whips and scorns of time,
Th' oppressor's wrong, the proud man's contumely,
The pangs of despised love, the law's delay,
The insolence of office, and the spurns
That patient merit of th' unworthy takes,
When he himself might his quietus make
With a bare bodkin? Who would fardels bear,
To grunt and sweat under a weary life,
But that the dread of something after death,
The undiscovered country, from whose bourn
No traveler returns, puzzles the will,
And makes us rather bear those ills we have,
Than fly to others that we know not of?

Thus conscience does make cowards of us all,
And thus the native hue of resolution
Is sicklied o'er with the pale cast of thought,
And enterprises of great pitch and moment,
With this regard their currents turn awry,
And lose the name of action. – Soft you now,
The fair Ophelia! – Nymph, in thy orisons
Be all my sins remembered.

RICHARD Let's talk of graves, of worms, and epitaphs.
Make dust our paper, and with rainy eyes
Write sorrow on the bosom of the earth.
Let's choose executors and talk of wills:
And yet not so, for what can we bequeath
Save our deposèd bodies to the ground?
Our lands, our lives, and all are Bolingbroke's,
And nothing can we call our own, but death
And that small model of the barren earth
Which serves as paste and cover to our bones.
For God's sake let us sit upon the ground
And tell sad stories of the death of kings:
How some have been deposed, some slain in war,
Some haunted by the ghosts they have deposed,
Some poisoned by their wives, some sleeping killed,
All murdered – for within the hollow crown
That rounds the mortal temples of a king
Keeps Death his court, and there the antic sits,
Scoffing his state and grinning at his pomp,
Allowing him a breath, a little scene,
To monarchize, be feared, and kill with looks,
Infusing him with self and vain conceit,
As if this flesh which walls about our life
Were brass impregnable; and, humored thus,
Comes at the last, and with a little pin
Bores thorough his castle wall, and farewell king!
Cover your heads, and mock not flesh and blood

With solemn reverence; throw away respect,
Tradition, form, and ceremonious duty;
For you have but mistook me all this while:
I live with bread like you, feel want,
Taste grief, need friends – subjected thus,
How can you say to me, I am a king?

HAMLET O that this too too sullied flesh would melt,
Thaw, and resolve itself into a dew,
Or that the Everlasting had not fixed
His canon 'gainst self-slaughter. O God, God,
How weary, stale, flat, and unprofitable
Seem to me all the uses of this world!
Fie on't, ah, fie, 'tis an unweeded garden
That grows to seed. Things rank and gross in nature
Possess it merely. That it should come to this:
But two months dead, nay, not so much, not two,
So excellent a king, that was to this
Hyperion to a satyr, so loving to my mother
That he might not beteem the winds of heaven
Visit her face too roughly. Heaven and earth,
Must I remember? Why, she would hang on him
As if increase of appetite had grown
By what it fed on; and yet within a month –
Let me not think on't; frailty, thy name is woman –
A little month, or ere those shoes were old
With which she followed my poor father's body
Like Niobe, all tears, why she, even she –
O God, a beast that wants discourse of reason
Would have mourned longer – married with my uncle,
My father's brother, but no more like my father
Than I to Hercules. Within a month,
Ere yet the salt of most unrighteous tears
Had left the flushing in her gallèd eyes,

She married. O, most wicked speed, to post
With such dexterity to incestuous sheets!
It is not, nor it cannot come to good.
But break my heart, for I must hold my tongue.

FEAR NO MORE THE HEAT O' TH' SUN

Fear no more the heat o' th' sun
   Nor the furious winter's rages;
Thou thy worldly task hast done,
   Home art gone and ta'en thy wages.
Golden lads and girls all must,
As chimney-sweepers, come to dust.

Fear no more the frown o' th' great;
   Thou are past the tyrant's stroke,
Care no more to clothe and eat;
   To thee the reed is as the oak.
The scepter, learning, physic, must
All follow this and come to dust.

Cymbeline, IV.ii.

EPILOGUE
Spoken by Prospero

Now my charms are all o'erthrown,
And what strength I have's mine own,
Which is most faint. Now 'tis true
I must be here confined by you,
Or sent to Naples. Let me not,
Since I have my dukedom got
And pardoned the deceiver, dwell
In this bare island by your spell;
But release me from my bands
With the help of your good hands.
Gentle breath of yours my sails
Must fill, or else my project fails,
Which was to please. Now I want
Spirits to enforce, art to enchant;
And my ending is despair
Unless I be relieved by prayer,
Which pierces so that it assaults
Mercy itself and frees all faults.
As you from crimes would pardoned be,
Let your indulgence set me free.

INDEX OF FIRST LINES

SPEECHES AND SONGS